Thoughts Are Not the Enemy

ALSO BY JASON SIFF

Unlearning Meditation

Thoughts Are
Not the Enemy

*An Innovative Approach
to Meditation Practice*

Jason Siff

Shambhala
Boston & London
2014

Shambhala Publications, Inc.
Horticultural Hall
300 Massachusetts Avenue
Boston, Massachusetts 02115
www.shambhala.com

9 8 7 6 5 4 3 2 1

First Edition
Printed in the United States of America

⊗This edition is printed on acid-free paper that meets the American National Standards Institute z39.48 Standard.
♲This book is printed on 30% postconsumer recycled paper.
For more information please visit www.shambhala.com.

Distributed in the United States by Penguin Random House LLC and in Canada by Random House of Canada Ltd

Designed by Daniel Urban-Brown

Library of Congress Cataloging-in-Publication Data

Siff, Jason.
Thoughts are not the enemy: an innovative approach to meditation practice / Jason Siff.—First edition.
pages   cm
Includes bibliographical references and index.
ISBN 978-1-61180-043-2 (paperback)
1. Meditation—Buddhism. 2. Meditation. I. Title.
BQ5612.S538 2014
294.3'4435—dc23
2013046153

In memory of my mother, Eileen Z. (Siff) Schnepp

Contents

PREFACE

An Innovative Approach to Meditation

An innovation is more than just something new—it is something at the cutting edge. I think many people today would say that mindfulness is at the cutting edge of meditation. Here, in this book, you will read about an approach to meditation that was developed out of my own practice of mindfulness meditation in the 1980s as a Buddhist monk in Sri Lanka. On the surface it focuses on developing a greater awareness of thoughts in meditation, but at its core, the direction is to form a broad awareness of everything that goes on in meditation: sensations, sense impressions, emotions, breathing, bodily awareness, memories, intentions, mental imagery, and, of course, thoughts.

Taken singly, some of the innovations may not strike you as anything new, but taken together, this meditation practice takes coherent form as something new and intriguing. The most provocative and challenging innovation, for most meditators, is the starting point for this new mindfulness of thinking: not stopping thoughts in meditation but allowing them to run their course. How that can be done skillfully, where it can effectively lead to tranquillity and insights, is the thrust of this approach to meditation.

In these pages, you will find enough meditation instruction to begin an open meditation practice, but you don't have to undertake such a practice to benefit from this book. In fact, you can read this book without ever meditating—the book itself will bring you into the minds of meditators, much like a good novel opens up the inner worlds of its characters and draws the reader into their lives. So whether you are an armchair meditator or a serious practitioner, my hope is that this book can further your exploration of your inner world and perhaps open up some new territories.

Jason Siff
Idyllwild, California
March 2013

Thoughts Are Not the Enemy

1

Thoughts Are Not the Enemy

I was driving down the highway the other day and thought about turning on the CD player. I felt an urge to listen to something other than my own thoughts. Then I paused and wondered what was so bad about listening to my thoughts. Earlier my thoughts were quite interesting and helped me with some work issues, so I didn't mind them as companions on this drive, but then my mind wandered to a movie I saw and some memories of my life as a teenager, and I began to feel shame about a mistake I'd made, and soon enough, there I was, itching to hear some music. Why did I want to distract myself from those thoughts? The obvious answer was that they were painful and would get the better of me and I would fear feeling miserable throughout the long drive. The less obvious answer was that I did not know how to be with those thoughts at that moment—I had forgotten how to listen to such thoughts.

A similar thing happened while I was meditating one day. My thoughts were focused on a topic I was going to write about, and then the direction turned south and I was thinking about an interaction I'd had with someone where I agreed to do something for that person that I didn't really want to do but felt obliged to do on account of our friendship. It seemed too big and complicated to sit with right then. But it kept coming back. I couldn't get any distance from it by noticing it or detaching from it or trying to quickly figure it out. No, this remembered interaction and my ambivalence about it were going to stay despite my wish for it to move on. And then I found my way to relate to it, and it stayed a little while longer, until it dissipated on its own.

We come to meditation to quiet our mind. This can be done by connecting with our thoughts rather than stopping our thoughts. It can be done by being in them and seeing what keeps them going. And it can be done in a kind and gentle way, requiring minimal effort.

So why isn't this approach to meditation commonly taught? Most people believe it won't work, so they never try it. They have been told that allowing thinking in meditation will lead to more thinking; that meditation is about getting out of the head and into the body; that you need to concentrate on a single object, such as the breath, in order for thoughts to die down; or that your true experience is beyond thought, transcending it completely. So they never let themselves think while meditating, and for them, thoughts become the enemy.

Thinking too much in meditation is made into a problem, when it really isn't one. It is just as natural to think about things, make plans, have fantasies, analyze, and problem solve while meditating as it is to feel your breath and body sensations. There is nothing wrong with thinking in meditation. You do it all the time outside of meditation, and then you are expected not to do it when you meditate—that is unnatural.

There seem to be two general types of thoughts that we don't want to have, especially when we are sitting in meditation. One type has to do with the thought's content—with the idea that such a thought is unacceptable for anyone meditating, and that even outside of meditation, it might be judged as evil, sinful, or unwholesome. Thoughts involving lust, violence, thieving, deceit, treachery, betrayal, envy, and grandiosity may feel as though they don't belong in meditation, and one may feel that immediate action must be taken to stop them. That is not the position I take. These thoughts can be allowed in meditation—getting to know them and seeing how they work may become an important feature of your meditation practice.

The other type of thought we may not want during meditation is considered unacceptable because of its process: it goes on and on without leading anywhere, and worse yet, it regularly comes back, even after a long absence. This is what meditators may refer to as discursive thought or derogatively as mental chatter or metaphorically as monkey mind. Many times these thoughts may be ordinary and mundane and essentially harmless, but they get a bad rap because they make it hard to focus on the breath or stay with the meditation instructions. But sometimes these recurrent thoughts have an obsessive quality to them, where they keep pounding away, begging you to listen and do something, making you feel anxious and confused. Instead of turning your attention away from these thoughts in meditation, allow them to go on.

If this were all it took for thoughts *not* to become your enemy in meditation, then there would be no need to write a book about it. You could simply sit and let yourself think in meditation. That is a good beginning. But that is not all of it. This is a journey, one that is more like an odyssey than a trip to the market. You will need a guide or, at the very least, a guidebook.

Let's take this slowly. Are you really ready to sit with your thoughts in meditation? Do you have reservations about it? Sure you do. I don't know anyone who doesn't. So as a first step I would like to invite you to attend one of my talks on this subject. I am giving it to a fictional Buddhist sangha and will begin after the first meditation sitting. If you like, you can meditate before moving on to the next section.

Bodhi Leaf Sangha Talk

I have been meditating for the past forty minutes and will have to ring the bell in five minutes, as I am the guest teacher tonight. The meditation hall is dark this Tuesday night in October, as the sun set half an hour ago and no one turned on the lights before the sitting started. There are about fifty people here tonight. I might know one or two, but the rest are new to me. I wonder how I will begin my talk, though I know the points I will cover:

1. Allowing thoughts and emotions into the meditation sitting from the outset is the only way for thinking not to become a problem in your meditation practice.
2. Maintaining a still sitting posture with the intention to meditate is enough restraint and effort to tolerate and become more aware of the thoughts and emotions you go through in a meditation sitting.
3. Gentleness and kindness toward your thoughts is necessary in order to develop awareness of them—otherwise you will tolerate them for only a short while before cutting them off.
4. When you are interested in your thoughts, there will be less aversion to them.
5. Becoming aware of thinking involves being in the thinking while it is going on and also experiencing moments of not being as embedded in it, where you can briefly reflect back on it.
6. Once your thoughts have died down, you will be more aware of other aspects of your experience, such as your breath.
7. And contrary to common beliefs, allowing your thinking in meditation leads to less thinking than not allowing it.

It is time to ring the bell. The low tone of the bell sends its sound through the meditation hall, jarring a couple of people, washing over everyone else, as they all slowly open their eyes and come out from their private inner worlds and enter into this public space, the meditation hall rented by the Bodhi Leaf Sangha from the local Unitarian church.

I am seated on my *zafu* on the linoleum floor. There are a few others also seated on cushions on the floor in front of me, but almost everyone is sitting in chairs. I ask the meditators to pause a couple of moments to reflect back on their meditation sitting before taking a break. A couple of people leave their seats, while everyone else obediently sits silently reflecting back on what happened during meditation. A few people pull out notepads and start writing. One young man types on his iPad.

After a couple of minutes I announce that we will take a ten-minute break. People start milling about, some talking to each other, while others are silent. There is a table with flyers for upcoming retreats led by various teachers, copies of a free Buddhist magazine, and sign-up sheets for people wishing to receive e-mails. In among all of this paper, there are two donation bowls, one for the Bodhi Leaf Sangha and the other for the guest speaker. I see a few people drop some dollar bills in the bowl for the sangha before they leave the building, having decided not to stay for the talk. What with their busy lives, I don't blame them.

The conversations get louder as more people stand up and walk around. On the surface, it is all very friendly. The woman in charge of tonight's meeting comes up to me to ask if I need anything before my talk. I'm fine with my glass of water and only request that the overhead lights be dimmed. "We'll begin in a couple of minutes," she says. "Should I ring the gong then?" I ask. She nods and I take that as a yes.

A few people look my way, disengaging momentarily from their conversations to see if I am about to put an end to this period of socializing. Even so, they go back into their conversations to keep the connection with another human being alive just a little longer.

I wait a couple of minutes before I ring the bell loudly, and then the room falls silent. People return to their seats. I wait for everyone to get settled, assuming that I will be beginning my talk soon. Instead, the woman leading the sangha this evening has a few announcements, which take a couple of minutes to get through. Then she introduces me, reading from her own handwriting on what looks like the back of some teacher's retreat flyer.

"Jason Siff is the author of *Unlearning Meditation: What to Do When the Instructions Get in the Way*. He was a Buddhist monk in Sri Lanka in the 1980s, left the order in 1990, and then studied counseling psychology and trained to become a psychotherapist, but he decided to devote himself to full-time meditation teaching in 1995. He founded the Skillful Meditation Project in 1996. He has yearly retreats at the Barre Center for Buddhist Studies, at Cloud Mountain Retreat Center, and at other retreat centers in the United States and Australia. He has developed his approach to meditation practice, called Recollective Awareness meditation, over the past twenty-five years."

What is always missing from these biographical introductions is the actual work I have done with meditation students. But only I can truthfully state how, for the past twenty-five years, hundreds of people have trusted me with their private inner world in meditation. I have read several thousand meditation journal entries, where people have shared in confidence their most personal thoughts, emotions, and experiences in meditation. In my own meditation practice, I have kept up a high level of self-honesty and have had to look at difficult and painful aspects of my mind, as well as reflect and accurately access any calm, peaceful, blissful state I might experience. I do not teach about enlightenment or any optimal state of mind, as that would go against what I most value about meditation practice: awareness of all states of mind.

Now I can begin. The words in my mind easily find their way across my vocal chords without hesitation.

"Thinking is an integral part of our experience. It won't just go away when we meditate. If we are honest with ourselves, much of our time in meditation is spent thinking. Even when you are trying to bring your attention back to the breath or follow your body sensations or stay with a mantra, there is still a good deal of thinking going on. This thinking then becomes a distraction, because it gets in the way of being more aware of the breath, of being more present.

"What this situation boils down to is conflict with your thoughts. Your thoughts become your enemy. In essence, you become your own enemy in meditation. Meditation becomes an exercise in eliminating the ego, ending selfhood, becoming empty of thoughts. A noble end, but this is no place to begin a meditation practice. All it leads to is forcefully stopping thoughts and more self-criticism and judgments for having thoughts.

"So how do you get to a place in your meditation practice where there is less self, less thinking, and more evenness, patience, kindness, and acceptance? How does such a practice begin?

"It begins by making your meditation practice a safe place for you to experience your thoughts and emotions. This kind of safety is fostered by knowing that when things get rough they can always bring their attention to their body, breath, or anything that gives a sense of stability and calm. For other people, safety may be found in having permission to do what they want in meditation, which may mean allowing thoughts and feelings to run their course. For others, a kind of safety is fostered by learning how to tolerate difficult and unpleasant emotions and thoughts. Yet others might find that becoming more aware of and interested in what is going on in meditation brings about a kind of openness to experiences that makes even the most troubling thoughts appear safe and manageable. And there may be combinations of these ways of creating a safe inner environment—along with other ways—that develop naturally in your meditation practice.

"What is not safe, however, is another story. Pushing yourself too hard in meditation does not create a safe environment. Stopping each thought when it arises . . . correcting your posture and micromanaging your experience . . . telling yourself you can do better or feel differently than you do . . . and replacing your 'negative' thoughts with positive affirmations are all like inviting a harsh and stern coach into your meditation world rather than a kind and friendly teacher."

I pause here to reflect on what I haven't said yet. I could go in a few different directions at this point. What I really want to do is stop here and respond to people's questions, but this talk would be considered too short. So I pick a theme that seems to me to follow up on what I last said.

"One of the main instructions I give is to be gentle with your harshness. Not to try to be gentle all the time, for that is artificial, but, rather, when you notice that you are being hard on yourself, pressuring yourself, to be kind and gentle to that harsh voice, that aggressive attitude.

"Along with that instruction, which I call a condition rather than an instruction, is the condition of interest. When you are kind to your harshness, then you may also find that you can become interested in it. It is like being with a loud and annoying child.... I recall once I was on an airplane and had obliged a single mother with three young children to have my window seat while I sat in the middle row next to her seven-year-old boy. This child was continually talking gibberish, calling me names when I didn't respond to him, and was not only irritating me but was bothering everyone around us. His mother attended to the other two children and rarely looked over. I didn't bargain for this when I gave up my seat. After half an hour of this kind of obnoxious behavior and my feeble attempts to reason with the boy, my friend Eoin, who was sitting a few rows down, came by to say hello. The boy looked up at him and started berating him, while Eoin affectionately put his hand on the child's shoulder and treated him in a genuinely friendly way. The boy settled down and Eoin had a short conversation with him, and I could then understand the boy's loneliness, his need for attention, and his fear, which were now coming out in ways that brought compassion instead of aversion. When I approached him with gentleness, I could become interested in this young boy's acting out and see that there was more to it than met the eye.

"In meditation practice we often try to get our mind to behave differently so that we can then know it. But maybe we don't let it 'act out' enough but clamp down on it too quickly, too forcefully, never giving it a chance to express itself. It is often because we have not cultivated the skillful means to be with whatever we are experiencing. In the same way, I had not developed the skillful means to be with that boy on the airplane, while my friend Eoin had.

"Eoin has young children and has had to find skillful ways to be with their crankiness, their irritation, their teasing, their rebelliousness—while I don't have children and have had little exposure to them as an adult. But I have had many meditation sittings where my mind was like an upset child, and now I had to move through my own dislike and impatience to find someplace where I could be of comfort to this child, could be trusted, could learn about what was going on, and could come to some kind of understanding and compassionate action. I just couldn't see the child on the plane like I see my mind in meditation—just as some people can't see their mind in meditation as like a child who is asking for attention.

"There is no technique, no strategy, for giving attention to thoughts in meditation. All the techniques do is either stop the thoughts or manage them in some way. Even a technique of observing your thoughts may not really give attention to them but, rather, encourage a kind of distancing from them. That is because meditation techniques treat thoughts as problems. When thinking is not a problem in meditation, then we can naturally become more aware of it.

"That is why I teach allowing thoughts and emotions into your meditation sitting from the very beginning. When someone starts meditating with thoughts not being a distraction, with their not being the enemy of concentration, a tolerant and accepting attitude toward thinking is fostered from the outset. With thoughts being tolerated in your meditation sitting, you will find you don't need some already-formed strategy to deal with them—you will find a way to relate to them that is skillful.

"How do I know that will happen? I am trusting in the development of certain qualities of mind that will enable you to be with and become interested in all kinds of thoughts and emotions. Qualities such as gentleness and kindness will be present, for that is how you are learning to relate to your thoughts. Patience with what is going on will also come to the fore, as will greater interest in your experience. But these qualities might be subtle and hard to detect, known by the absence of harshness, impatience, or lethargy."

I decide to pause and take a sip of water. I recall the seven points I wanted to cover in this talk and feel that I have done justice to most of them, but I am also reminded that I have overlooked one in particular that would fit in well here. So I continue.

"I define meditation as what happens when you intend to meditate. Whatever follows from the intention to meditate is meditation. So all you need to do is adopt the posture you use for meditation and decide to meditate for the activity to be called meditation. That posture provides enough restraint to prevent you from immediately acting on your thoughts or emotions. It enables you to tolerate them, knowing that they are within your mind and not going out into the world. The intention to meditate operates in the background, so that you can allow unwholesome thoughts and emotions to go on, knowing that you are not doing so in order to indulge in them and be won over by them but to get to know them more thoroughly. You are allowing your inner world to reveal itself to you as it is. And meditating in this way provides enough safety for that to happen.

"But if you get overwhelmed by certain thoughts and emotions, you can always bring your attention to something that you find grounding. I would suggest bringing your attention to your body sitting still, most particularly to your hands resting in your lap or to your feet or legs touching the floor, your mat, or your chair. But don't keep your attention there—instead, use it like a perch, a resting place, and then let the thoughts and emotions that were overwhelming return if they like. In that way you will develop greater tolerance for those thoughts and emotions and, in time, will most likely feel less overwhelmed by them.

"An important feature of this approach to meditation is choice. There are many moments in your meditation sitting where you can make a choice. Instead of always making the same choice, such as always bringing your attention back to your breath, make choices that you haven't made before in meditation. Choose to follow a thought that keeps begging for attention or let yourself drift toward sleep instead of trying to wake yourself up, or choose to be with sounds, smells, sensations. You have permission to do what you would like in meditation—you don't have to do any prescribed practice or even anything I suggest. Your meditation practice is your own affair."

It seems that this is a good place to end. I feel fine about this talk, and I hope it communicates well what I teach. But I never really know for sure until I hear people's questions.

I project my voice, making sure everyone can hear. "That is about all I have to say in this talk. Would anyone like to ask a question?"

As I mentioned, there are a few people seated on cushions in front of me, but the majority of people are seated in four rows of chairs. A middle-aged woman in the first row raises her hand, and I call on her.

She asks, "You say that allowing thinking will lead to less thinking. But when one thought prompts another, isn't that leading to more thinking?"

When someone asks a question based on the person's own observation of his or her experience, I would be the last person to argue against it.

"That is a good question," I reply. "It is true that one thought may prompt another and push your thinking along, leading to more thinking. What I am talking about is creating an inner mental environment where there will be less thinking overall. Most practices aim at reducing or eliminating thinking in the moment. That is the bias in many meditation instructions—they are meant to accomplish something right now, at the moment you use them—while the approach I've just described utilizes cultivation of certain qualities of mind that, over time, will reduce thinking. But in the moment, one can see that by not being harsh with one's thoughts, there are fewer negative thoughts and unpleasant feelings about the thoughts you are having."

A fellow sitting next to the woman raises his hand. He is thin, bald, and looks to be in his late sixties. His plaid shirt is newly pressed, and he seems to be tidy and self-conscious about his appearance.

He asks, "You don't seem to agree with the practice of settling your mind on the in and out breath before bringing your attention to thoughts. Why is that?"

I don't recall bringing up that point in the talk. Perhaps he read this on my website.

I reply, "When people settle their mind before allowing thoughts in meditation, they do not get to know their thoughts and emotions as they would normally arise. They encounter a more manageable and diminished form of those thoughts and emotions and many times may even find it hard to be aware of thoughts because they don't have many thoughts when their mind gets settled. Such awareness of thoughts and emotions may be helpful at those times, but since the thinking is not at its usual intensity, this awareness may not carry over into awareness of thoughts in daily life. The person may still have difficulty tolerating and being interested in thoughts occurring at their normal volume and intensity. What I am suggesting is a way to become aware of thoughts and emotions at their normal volume and intensity, which can be carried on outside meditation, though it may be initially developed within meditation."

The gentleman seems not to be wholly satisfied with my answer but then drops that topic to ask another question: "By not bringing your attention back to the breath, how do you develop concentration?"

It then occurs to me that he must practice awareness of breathing and wants to make sure that I understand the value of that kind of practice. It can settle the mind and create concentration. I don't disagree.

"With awareness of breathing, you develop concentration by holding your attention on the breath. With this approach, you develop concentration through clearing away the hindrances to concentration. Focusing on the breath is a more direct way to become concentrated, but I believe that such concentration is often short-lived and fragile, because one has taken a shortcut to get there. Becoming concentrated through attending to the hindrances is an indirect way—and may be the long way around—but it is a sure way. When you have been sitting with thoughts about sense gratification, which is one of the five hindrances, and have listened to them, understood them, become less driven by them, then your mind may drop that hindrance and find itself in a calmer, more settled state. In this instance, concentration comes out of tranquillity, which is arrived at through awareness of thoughts and emotions, rather than the other way around, where you are concentrating on the breath in order to enter into a tranquil state."

A young woman, at least for this crowd, who may be in her forties, with long blond hair and a pleasant, round face speaks up as I finish that last sentence.

She asks, "How is this different from daydreaming?"

I get asked this a lot. Usually I feel the person has not understood what I have been saying, but then again, it may be difficult to see the difference between awareness of thoughts and emotions as I teach it and common daydreaming.

I say, "The difference lies in the intention to meditate. You can daydream and ruminate in your meditation sitting, but it won't be quite the same as it would be outside of meditation. When you are not meditating, it is more likely you will just go with the thoughts and not try to notice anything about them, like what keeps them going, what they are dependent on, or how you are relating to them. You will just be thinking them. In meditation you can learn how to look into the process of thinking without stopping your thoughts or trying to distance yourself from them; that experience will at times feel as if you were "just thinking them"—for that is what you are doing—but you are doing it in the service of letting the thoughts reveal themselves more fully and for getting a perspective on them that enables you to explore them. I can't say it any more clearly, as any way of saying it right now is going to be abstract. If you try this out in your meditation sittings over time, you may have experiences that confirm this better than anything else I might say about it."

I feel I have said a bit too much by the end of the answer. Yet I do want to stress in my talks that finding what I am saying in your own experience will confirm this approach much more than my trying to convince you about it.

"Another question," I say. I look around the room and, seeing no hands raised, incorrectly conclude that no one is eager to talk.

"I have one," a woman seated in the second row says. She stands up to deliver her question. She is wearing large gold earrings that reflect light into my eyes, which I find distracting.

"I like what you are saying and think I have been doing some of what you are talking about. But I can't see how becoming interested in mundane thoughts is going to go anywhere. Shouldn't these thoughts just be noticed and discarded?"

I reply, "If you haven't let mundane thoughts go on in your meditation sitting, then you might experiment with allowing and following such thoughts. When such thoughts are noticed, there is often a value judgment placed on them: they are worthless, they don't lead anywhere, or they are just a waste of time. The only way to see if this is true is to experiment with allowing them. You may not be able to fully allow some mundane or trivial thoughts, but there may be others you can. Then start with those.

"My experience has been that we often don't know where a train of thought will lead at its outset. So when we judge it at the beginning as worthless or mundane, we are operating on very limited knowledge of it. We may know only that it is, for example, a plan to buy something, say a piece of jewelry, and at first you think that is all the thought is about. But then it comes back a couple of times and you decide to listen to it, let it open itself up to you, and you have thoughts about how the earrings will look on you, where you will wear them, how wearing them will make you feel—will they draw too much attention and embarrass you, or will they flatter you? In this process you can explore the desire that supports the plan and the sense of self that supports the desire, which gives you more insight and knowledge into yourself and the way your mind works than just knowing that you were planning to buy a pair of earrings."

This last reply was much longer than I intended. I hope that I didn't offend her by talking about earrings in my example, but I just latched on to it. Perhaps I didn't need an example and could have let my answer be abstract. Or maybe I drew her attention to something of direct use for her that she was more than ready to hear. I will probably never know.

I do feel as if I have answered enough questions for the night and hope there are no more. I check the clock and see that there are five minutes left. These evening groups often don't mind ending a few minutes early. I am about to suggest that we end here when I see a hand go up in the second row. It is a young man in his mid-twenties wearing glasses and with short-cropped hair. I notice that he has a tattoo in Devanagari script on his right forearm, and I momentarily try to focus on it so that I can decipher what it says.

He asks, "You keep referring to exploring your experiences in meditation. How is that actually done? You seem to be saying something different from asking questions or bringing in ideas or issues to think about in the meditation sitting."

"That's right," I say. This young man may have read my most recent book, or else he has been listening closely all evening.

"I am talking about a receptive, open-ended kind of exploration, one that comes out of being with your experience and is not imposed upon it. Some people find themselves doing this kind of exploration quite naturally, as when they start contemplating something that has come up in the meditation sitting. Others may not have experienced something like this and have relied on asking prescribed questions such as 'Who am I?' or 'What is this?' When you inquire into your experience with already-formed questions, there is often some pressure, some wish, some need to get an answer or to get closer to an answer. With an open-ended exploration, the need for resolution, for the investigation to culminate in a realization, is not present. You are following your own observations, coming up with your own questions, occasionally finding the more correct or more clearly understood idea, which is treated as useful and insightful for now but not the final answer. Instead of seeking an end to the exploration, you are developing your skills at discernment—that is, you are becoming able to have more nuanced understandings of subtler aspects of your experience. This, I believe, is necessary for us to begin seeing our experience more as it has arisen than as what we have led ourselves to believe about it through our faulty narratives.

"I could say more about this, but it seems that we have reached the end of the time for this talk. Thank you all for coming and listening to me speak this evening."

I clasp my hands in front of my chest and bow to everyone. All of them do the same to me. I smile for a couple of moments, and most everyone smiles back, and then I get up and everyone else rises and prepares to leave, though, as usual, a few people come up to me after the talk.

A woman who was sitting quietly in the second row approaches me. She is tall and thin, in her sixties, with short gray hair, glasses, and a rather narrow but handsome face. She has an aura of being very serious and direct.

"I have been practicing your approach since I read your book in March," she says. "It has been very helpful. I was very much attached to meditating on my breath, and now I have such lightness and freedom in my meditation sittings."

"That's good to hear," I say.

She continues, "I wanted to ask you if I could send you my meditation journals and get some guidance from you."

"Yes, of course," I say. "You can e-mail me your meditation journal entries and I will reply with some times that we can talk on the phone or Skype. We would talk for half an hour or so. Do you have my e-mail?"

"No, but could you sign my copy of your book and include your address?"

"Certainly." I take her book and write a short inscription and give her my e-mail address.

"I'm very happy that you are willing to do this for me," she says.

"I do it all the time," I respond.

The person behind her seems to be anxious to ask me a question. She is the woman who asked the first question, the one about one thought leading to another.

"I suffer from obsessive thinking," she tells me, "and I have never been able to meditate long without being plagued with unwanted thoughts. Do you have any advice for me?"

"Do you usually start off the sitting with bringing your attention to your breath?"

"Yes, that is how I have been taught."

"Try not doing that for a while. Just let yourself go into the meditation sitting with the thoughts you are having. When you start obsessing, listen to the tone of voice in the thoughts, the rhythm of the thoughts, the mood or attitude in and around the thoughts. Be gentle with your thoughts. It is okay to think these thoughts in meditation."

"What if I get overwhelmed by them?"

"I know you are afraid of these thoughts going on too long and becoming intense. Acknowledge that fear and be kind to it. It is all right to have these thoughts while you meditate and to make them part of your meditation rather than as things to get rid of."

"Will they go away?"

"I don't know," I say truthfully. "What I do know is that you will become less averse to them and find your own way to be with them."

"Thank you," she says, with a tear forming at her right eye.

I too feel her sadness and her relief. Along with that, I feel my exhaustion from the night. So I pack up my cushion and collect my watch, bell, and voice recorder and make my way out of the building and into the parking lot. On my way to my car, I say good-bye to one person after another, sharing a smile, not knowing whether I will ever see any of them again.

2

Meditating with Thoughts and Emotions

It is easy to see the value in making the breath the object of one's meditation. Focusing on the breath can lead to calmness, to less involvement in obsessive thoughts, to quiet and peace, and to being more present in one's body. The breath is also a simple phenomenon to observe. It goes in and comes out, one breath following another, with a gap between each cycle. There are lessons to be found in observing it that are clear and, upon first encounter, profound. Also, we trust that being aware of the breath will lead somewhere good and wholesome, whereas being aware of our thoughts and emotions as they present themselves to us—well, we trust them less. There's good reason that breath awareness has become such a popular meditation method.

When it comes to being aware of emotions as something distinct from thoughts, you may have more confidence that it will lead somewhere. A good deal of psychotherapy is about being with your emotions, either facing them or learning how to express them appropriately. Often when you are instructed to pay attention to emotions in meditation, it is as physical sensations. You are instructed to notice the anxiety in your chest and how that sensation feels. By staying with the physical sensation and focusing on it, the emotion within the sensation may become manageable and go away. In this way you are looking at the bodily manifestation of the emotion but not the mental manifestation of it, as is found in the thoughts that accompany it.

How would emotions manifest in your thoughts? Most obviously, the emotions manifest in the tone of voice, the attitude that is in the verbal thinking. You may be able to identify a person's voice in the thoughts. It may not always be your own. You can focus on the tone of the voice, the rhythm of the words and phrases, the choice of words. An emotion within a train of thought is not just a disembodied feeling—it is fused to a person that is either you or someone who has gotten into your head (not literally, but it can feel as though that person were talking through your thoughts).

Even if you can't detect any emotions in your thoughts, your thoughts are rarely ever disembodied voices. Thinking does involve your body in some way. But your experience may not always be of your physical body—it may be of a form your mind creates from which it thinks. This is the notion of an inner self or higher self. That self feels as though it has a location, somewhere it resides. It keeps speaking from there. When it has your voice, it may feel more like you; when it has someone else's manner of speaking, you may think it is coming from outside of you, but the location of the voice may be the same. Locating your inner voice in the head or the heart or somewhere in between (the throat) does not provide the answer to the questions "Where does this voice come from? Where does it originate?" It leads us in the wrong direction in trying to understand the sources of our ways of thinking. For some people, this view of finding where thoughts come from leads to practices of holding one's attention on the area in one's head, heart, or throat and trying to catch the emergence of thoughts. And if one can't catch them in the moment, then one may try to trace them back to their physical abode. This is not looking at thinking as thinking—it is looking at it exclusively in the body.

The source of present thoughts is past actions of thought, speech, and body. If you have a certain voice that you use when you complain about others, then that voice may appear in your thoughts. If you have yelled at people in the past for not doing things right (that is, the way you want), then you may find an inner voice that yells at people, including you, in your head. This is what happens in meditation: we tend to experience our outer voices as inner ones. We repeat the same actions of speech and body that we let go on unchecked and unexamined in our life, and so it is with thoughts within meditation. These are thoughts that keep on going, and seemingly won't go away.

The way for thinking to quiet down more reliably is through allowing and tolerating it. But that may not happen by *trying* to allow your thinking and *trying* to tolerate it. Effort gets in the way— it is like a coach who pushes you so hard that he throws you off your game. You know how to sit and think, you have been doing it much of your life, so all you have to do here is intentionally adopt a meditation posture for a period of time in which you just let your mind do what it naturally does.

We all know how to be lazy, but many of us have too much guilt around it. If that is you, you will need to become more passive with thoughts and emotions—do nothing about them. Let yourself, for a change, be lazy, unfocused, undisciplined, passive. This is how you will learn to be receptive to your mind *as it is*.

Receptivity is a progressive step that can develop out of passivity. The difference between receptivity and passivity is that passivity has the sense of being swept along and under the complete sway of another. While receptivity also entails being swept along, it does not move in the direction of being controlled by another; there is a sense of going along with, and also of noticing what is going on and being able to make a choice.

Allowing your thinking to go on and on is going to meet up with resistance. Even without trying, you will interrupt, clip, stop, and push away certain thoughts and emotions. It is most likely you will not accept many of your thoughts and emotions. But you may learn to tolerate a few of the thoughts and emotions you cannot accept.

That is why I prefer the word *tolerate* to the word *accept* when talking about becoming receptive and open to one's experience. It is realistic for us to become more tolerant, that is, to be able to sit with difficult emotions and still want to push them away or get through them. You can do that. You can learn to sit with long trains of uncomfortable thoughts and emotions for a bit longer than usual. No one is asking you to sit with what you cannot even begin to tolerate, just what you can slowly begin to tolerate.

The Minds of Meditators

I have tried to convey what goes on in the minds of meditators using various forms of writing. Each form has its advantages and disadvantages. With nonfiction, I have primarily used the journals of meditation students, as I did in my previous book, *Unlearning Meditation*. The journal entries used in that book have the advantage of being honest recollections of actual meditation sittings. But such journals often require some kind of "decoding" and commentary to make sense to general readers. They also do not have the kind of immediacy of experience that is necessary to get a feel for what I am talking about. Meditation, if anything else, is immediate. So I have decided to start off with some fictional stream-of-consciousness meditation sittings. I assure you that these are true-to-life depictions of what goes on during actual meditation sittings—just the down-to-earth experiences of ordinary meditators. You may even recognize some things that happen to you when you sit.

Two First-Time Students

Becky had never meditated before in her life and came to one of my workshops because she had heard from a friend that it might make her calm. She is in her sixties, retired, divorced, and is mostly involved in volunteer work and taking care of her two dogs and three cats. She tried yoga and read some Eastern philosophy in college but never stuck with it. She is curious to see what this kind of Buddhist meditation would do for her.

There is a group of about twenty people seated in the meditation hall. I begin by giving meditation instructions to everyone: "You have permission to do the meditation practice you have been doing. You also have permission not to do it. The choice is up to you. At any point during the sitting, you can stop doing the practice you usually do and do another practice you would like to do, or you can try the beginning instructions I am about to give.

"Sit in a comfortable posture, one that you will not need to change for the twenty minutes of this first sitting. If you do need to move, do so slowly and mindfully." I demonstrate what I mean by that, lifting my right foot off my left knee, as I am sitting in a half lotus, and gently moving it onto the cushion in front of me, and then tucking it under my left knee. I continue, "You can bring your attention to the feel of your hands touching each other in your lap or your feet contacting the floor or your cushion or your rear against your chair. Just be aware of the external contact of your body touching something. But do not hold your attention there. Instead, allow your thoughts and feelings into the meditation sitting."

Then I elaborate a bit, saying, "Do not hold your attention on the external contact points. Just bring your attention there if you feel you need to, such as when some thinking has gone on too long or some emotions have become too intense. And when you bring your attention to the contact points, hold it there for just a few seconds and then allow your mind to go where it will."

Lastly, I add, "If you feel sleepy, let yourself go toward sleep. If you feel restless, that is okay, just sit with it. However, if you need to get up and leave, you can, but if so, don't return to the hall until the sitting is over."

I ask the person sitting near the light switch to turn down the lights, and then we sit in silence for twenty minutes.

BECKY'S MIND IN MEDITATION

"Bring my attention to my hands, that's what he said." She brings her attention to her hands folded in her lap and moves the fingertips of the lower hand gently across the knuckles of the other hand resting on top.

"My left thumb rests on my right forefinger and my right thumb rests on top of the left thumb. I remember seeing pictures of Buddhas sitting with the tips of their thumbs touching. I should try that." She moves her hands a little farther apart and then raises her thumbs to touch each other at their tips.

"This feels a bit strange now—the two tips pressed together produces a rather uncomfortable sensation. I am not sure I like it. But I should just stop fidgeting and get into the meditation sitting."

After about a minute, the sensations at the tips of her thumbs feel like the previous sensations of one hand touching the other. She doesn't realize how quiet the room has been until the forced-air heater turns on.

"That sure is loud. I wonder if I will be able to concentrate with all of this noise. Good thing the heater is across the room. I can hear someone moving about near it. It sounds like someone is lying down. I wish I could open my eyes to find out."

She keeps her eyes closed, though she imagines seeing a slender thirtyish woman lying down on her back. She noticed this woman while the teacher was giving meditation instructions. She was sitting across the room, near the point of the heater sound, and had a yoga mat under her meditation cushion.

"That woman probably brought that yoga mat so that she can lie down. I don't blame her. I would like to lie down."

She feels a bit tired at the moment. Her hands feel heavier, and the touch sensation between them has vanished. They seem fused together. "I wonder if my hands have fallen asleep. Is that even possible? Perhaps I should wiggle my fingers a little." She thinks about moving her fingers but doesn't. She realizes that it is not possible for her hands to become fused, even though she is imagining it's happening.

Her attention is glued to the physical sensation of heaviness in her hands, and a vivid image appears of two large white marble hands positioned like hers. She is startled.

"What was that? It looked like a Buddha carved out of marble. Where have I seen that before? In a book? I doubt it. This meditation is very strange . . . ; I'd like to open my eyes and get oriented."

She brings her attention to her eyes, but they don't open. She becomes aware of a very subtle sensation of her eyelids touching. After a few seconds that vanishes and it feels as though her eyes were now fused shut. She is not afraid of it and so does not struggle with it. Instead she lets herself drift toward sleep. Soon her head is hanging down with her chin touching her chest. She hears the bell ending the twenty-minute sitting. It reverberates gently, rousing her to the surface.

"Well, that was relaxing."

JILL'S MIND IN MEDITATION

It turns out that there is another first-time meditator at this workshop, though she really doesn't consider herself one, since she had attended a guided meditation workshop a year ago. Her name is Jill and she is a lawyer in her midforties. Her therapist recommended that she attend this workshop. It might help her with her anxiety, though Jill is skeptical of that. As she listens to the meditation instructions, she wonders what she has gotten herself into here. She believes she can't sit still for twenty minutes, even in the most comfortable chair, let alone this wooden dining room chair she is sitting on. She moves to the edge of the chair and firmly plants her stocking feet on the rough carpeting. When the instructions are over, she feels determined to keep her attention on the soles of her feet throughout the meditation.

"I mustn't get anxious here, but I already feel anxious. How am I going to make it through this sitting? I can't just let my thoughts go all over the place for twenty minutes. I need to be able to rein in my thoughts. This just isn't for me."

She sighs and brings her attention down to her feet. She can feel her right foot more than the left one. Her right heel digs into the carpet more forcefully, and there is a sensation of tightness extending along her calf. Once she becomes aware of the tightness, she tries to relax it.

"Where does this tension in my leg come from? I have never

known it to be this tight. I wonder where else I'm holding tension."

She moves her attention up both of her legs and into her belly and chest. She finds a vibrating sensation at the center of her chest.

"This feels like a knot. It also feels like breathing ice-cold air. But then at the center of it is a kind of buzzing, like there is a bee in my chest."

She focuses her attention like a laser beam on the buzzing sensation. It seems to get bigger, more diffuse, as if it were shaking apart as it grows. And poof! It's gone. Her whole body feels lighter, and there is less tension in her mind.

"That was strange! I wonder what happened. But I feel quite a bit calmer. I still don't know what I am going to do for the rest of the meditation sitting. There must be at least fifteen minutes left. I could sit here and think about work, my husband, or what I am going to do for the rest of the weekend, but that wouldn't be meditation. I'm not sure what sitting here feeling my feet and butt will do."

She brings her attention to her rear perched on the edge of the chair. She slides back a little into the seat of the chair and straightens her back, making sure it doesn't touch the backrest.

"There, that feels good. What else can I be aware of?"

She then brings her attention to the sounds in the room. A moment later, the forced-air furnace turns on, which startles her slightly, and then it blends into the background.

"I'm surprised I'm not getting anxious. There are so many things in my life that demand attention. I am always behind, trying to catch up. I'm surprised I'm having these thoughts without getting anxious."

She brings her attention to her chest in search of a sensation akin to anxiety but doesn't find one. She moves her attention to her breath and finds that it is slow and steady and not anxious in the least. But she knows there is something in her experience that has the flavor of anxiety; she just can't put her finger on it.

"I really have to stop getting myself all in a tizzy. Whenever I think about what I need to be doing, what I should be doing right now instead of sitting here doing nothing, I feel this rush of energy literally blowing my sails." She then pictures an old schooner with its sails filled out by the wind.

"There is something like the wind that pushes my thinking forward. It blows in and fills me with pressures. I wish I could get underneath it, see what causes it. But I don't know if that is what I should be doing in meditation. And if that is what I should be doing, how should I do it? This meditation thing is so confusing. I really don't know what I should be doing. How much time is left?"

She wants to open her eyes to see the time but restrains herself. Instead she twiddles her thumbs in some kind of pantomime of impatience.

"I do wish he would ring the bell. Surely twenty minutes has passed. I really don't know how I am going to do this for the rest of the time. I could plan my workweek."

This sounds like the right thing to do, so she jumps right into it: "On Monday I will set up the conference call between K and D and maybe we can negotiate an agreement without their meeting in person. They just don't get along. K says something and D reacts, which gets K to react, and off they go into another fight. I just can't let that happen again."

She notices some fear of these two people as she thinks about them and then turns her attention toward the fear.

"I'm afraid of what will happen if I am in the room with both of them again. I mustn't let that happen. Good. That's decided. I'm no longer anxious about that at least."

In the middle of that last thought she heard the bell ring. It didn't interrupt the thought however. She is grateful that she can now open her eyes and get up off the chair.

A Recollective Awareness Meditator

Another person who is attending this workshop for the past two months is a forty-year-old man by the name of Mark. He has attended one of my workshops before. He started with mindfulness meditation about three years ago and was at first quite skeptical of

Recollective Awareness. The only reason he tried it was that his wife of ten years, Jessica, was initially introduced to this approach and wanted him to experience it for himself. In his daily sittings, he likes to alternate between mindfulness meditation and Recollective Awareness meditation. The distinction he makes between these two practices is that when he sits down to practice mindfulness, he returns to the breath whenever his mind wanders, while with Recollective Awareness he feels he can let his mind wander much longer without having to bring it back to the breath. So today he intends to practice Recollective Awareness all day long.

MARK'S MIND IN MEDITATION

"Today I will let my mind go and be gentle with it. It's not hard. But first I will bring my attention to the breath so as to get settled."

He brings his attention to his breath at the nostrils. It feels smooth and regular. He doesn't note whether it is in or out; he is simply aware that a breath occurred. Thoughts come in to interrupt his concentration on the breath, and he stops each thought before it builds momentum. "Jessica was excited about today." He stops that thought and returns to the breath, catching the air going in as it tickles his right nostril. "I forgot my lunch." He stops that thought and searches for the breath, finding it in his lungs. "I think I saw that guy sitting over in the corner at a sangha meeting." He stops that thought and reminds himself to return to the breath but doesn't do it. "I wonder why my mind is so active this morning." He stops that thought and wishes he could just be with the breath, but he can't find it anywhere. "I wish it would settle down." He listens to that thought and becomes aware that he has been trying to get his mind to settle down by forcefully stopping thoughts.

"Wasn't I going to practice Recollective Awareness today? If I am going to do that practice, I need to stop stopping my thoughts. I will just have to endure the thinking without getting calm first. So here I am, welcoming my thoughts. Let them come."

He straightens his back and does a brief body scan, his attention going down his trunk to his waist and then along his crossed legs, and then back to the shoulders and down each arm.

"My body feels good today, so today's sittings should be good too. I really hope I can sit with all of this thinking today, because it doesn't seem to be going away. I remember a few sittings where I was allowing thinking to go on and after a while it started to dissipate. I hope that will happen today. I don't know why thinking in meditation is scary at times like this. Maybe because I'm not thinking about anything important—I'm just thinking to think. It is like talking and talking with nothing really to say. I can see why people call this mental chatter."

He brings his attention back to his body sitting and becomes aware of his posture. There is something still and stable about his body. He wishes his mind would be like that.

"I am still troubled by this whole notion of following your thoughts and not seeking pure experience. My mind keeps taking me away from what is calm and still, but I believe that if I try to hold my mind on the calm and still body sitting, it will become so."

He brings his attention back to his body posture, doing another quick scan. It doesn't seem as still to him this time. There is agitation in the chest and limbs. It feels like an emotion.

"What is this feeling? Is it sadness? Is it rage? I frankly can't tell what it is. I could burst out either crying or screaming at somebody. I am so tightly wound! This is getting unbearable."

His attention is now strongly focused on the agitation in his chest. He wants to break down the sensation into smaller and smaller parts. This has helped in the past.

"If I could only get this sensation to dissolve, I would feel fine. But I'm not concentrated enough and it doesn't want to change! I don't really know what else to do. I feel really crummy."

He moves his attention back to his whole body sitting, and the agitation in his chest feels as if it were being watched from a distance.

"I have heard Jason talk about looking at the underlying mood in the experience. This definitely has a mood to it. It is sad, fearful, and raging. It is also restless, agitated, and unpleasant." Each of these words describes a facet of what he is feeling. He holds this description in his mind as his attention goes from his whole body to his chest, and a word keeps appearing in relation to it: *sad*.

"I can let myself be sad. I am sad about many things in my life, and I never spend time with my sadness. I am always trying to control it, to stop it. But what am I really sad about? So many things: lost opportunities, things not working between me and Jess, my lack of success at my age, and no sense of real purpose. I don't want to think about these things."

He brings his attention back to his whole body sitting, but instead of doing a body scan, he lets his attention rest on the contact of his legs touching the cushion. His legs feel as if they merge into the soft cotton cushion. The sadness is no longer lodged in his torso but spreads throughout his whole body. One moment he is feeling very heavy and down, and in the next, as if a knife had cut through the mood, he feels light and relaxed.

"Ahhh! That feels good."

A Recollective Awareness Meditator

Jessica is in her late thirties and has been meditating for one year. She started with Recollective Awareness meditation, not having tried meditation before. She had ideas about what meditation should be, mostly from listening to her husband, Mark. From what she heard, she felt that mindfulness was not for her. When she heard from a friend that a Recollective Awareness meditation workshop was being offered in her area, she thought she would like to try it. She has stuck with this approach, meditating four or five times a week, usually sitting for forty minutes. She attended a five-day retreat two months ago, and this is her first workshop since the retreat.

Jessica's Mind in Meditation

"I'll start by bringing my attention to my hands folded in my lap. I always liked that instruction."

With her attention on her hands, she also notices the sounds in the room of people getting into their meditation position and the traffic noise from a busy street a couple of blocks away.

"I wonder what Mark is doing in his meditation. I hope he can loosen up today and maybe get in touch with his feelings. That would be good. I shouldn't think about him—this is for me. But if I am thinking about him, then that is what I'm thinking about."

She brings her attention back to her hands and is aware that she did that because she didn't want to go on thinking about her husband. She recognizes a little fear in her chest.

"I really don't want to go into my relationship with Mark today. It is exhausting. And I have been avoiding it all week." The fear grows stronger, and she can feel it in her head. "I can't avoid it anymore. Here it is. I'm afraid we can't heal our wounds, repair the flaws in our relationship, that it is over."

She becomes more anxious after having allowed these thoughts.

"I just don't know what I will do. I can't just leave him without talking about it. How could I leave him? It's just not possible."

Her mind is racing with thoughts. The fear has moved into the background, though it is still present in her body.

"I could stay with my mother, my sister, but not my brother and his wife. I would rather stay with friends. Which ones? Sue, Jenny, Ann, Crystal, or Lisa? I don't want to impose on any of them. I haven't even told anyone that we are having problems, so how could I impose on anyone? I would look like some irrational crazy woman, and they would all tell me to see a therapist and try to work it out. These are crazy thoughts, because I am certainly not going to leave my husband today or any other day. I must try to work things out."

This last thought changes the direction in her thinking. "I tense up when I am around him. I want to talk about things that are going on between us, but I can't seem to get up the courage to do so. I have this picture of him dismissing me or yelling at me if I bring up something uncomfortable in our relationship."

She imagines Mark turning away from her as she brings up one of her grievances. But the image doesn't quite look like him. It looks more like her father.

"I don't recall Mark ever turning away like that. He might look away, but he stays seated and is with me when I have something to tell him. But my father would leave the room whenever my mother brought up a complaint or said something he didn't like. I don't think they ever really talked anything through. Maybe that is why I am scared to bring up discord with Mark. What have I been holding on to here?"

Her attention moves of its own accord to her chest, where now she feels a tight knot but no fear. The knot is interesting to her, and she focuses on it. As she does, she starts to think: "I have been holding on to the habit of running away instead of facing things. It's just happening again. It seems to start with my avoiding something that has been bothering me. Then I finally try to face it and I get scared. When I'm afraid, I start to catastrophize and make frantic plans, as if the plans would prevent the catastrophe from happening. I've just begun to overthink it, but the first part is right."

She can feel the knot loosen. Her attention stays with the knot in her chest, and a vivid picture of a pretzel arises. She is startled by it.

"That is not the kind of knot I was thinking of. But it will do."

She smiles inwardly. She straightens her posture and brings her attention to the touch of the hands. Her mind moves on to other trains of thought for the rest of the meditation sitting.

After the Meditation Sitting

I strike my seven-metal singing bowl with a padded wooden striker, and the bowl emits a midrange sound that is not jarring. Some people open their eyes sooner than others, and when everyone's eyes are open, the lights are turned up. I ask everyone to reflect back on their meditation sitting and see what they remember about it. After a couple of minutes, I begin giving instructions on keeping a meditation journal.

"In your meditation journal, try to write a description of what happened in your own words. If you have thoughts about the sitting while you are writing, put those in brackets. What we are looking for is an honest and faithful description of what occurred during the meditation sitting.

"At the beginning of your journal entry, write the length of the meditation period and the day it occurred. The description can be as short as a single paragraph and as long as a couple of pages. Some people prefer to write down experiences in numbered lists, while others may prefer to create a mind map, diagramming in a creative way what occurred during the sitting. Whatever method works for you is fine.

"When recalling the meditation sitting, it is advisable to begin with what you remember most clearly. Once you have written that down, you may find that other parts of the meditation period will come back to mind, and then you can easily write them down. Doing it in this way will generally lead to events in the sitting being written out of order, so you may decide to put it in order later on, though that is not really necessary."

To give you some idea of what someone's journal entry might look like, we can look over Jessica's shoulder as she writes down her sitting in her meditation journal.

SATURDAY, MARCH 3, 2012 (20 MINUTES)

I began with awareness of sounds. I was trying not to think about my marriage, but that is what my mind wanted to pursue, so I let it. I felt some fear in my chest. At first it was mild, but it grew stronger, and I began to think about what I would do if I left my husband [I hope he never reads this journal]. I was afraid to talk to him about our relationship. I thought he would turn away like my father would with my mother. But then I realized that he is not like my father. I felt a knot in my chest after the fear left. I stayed with that sensation and saw a picture of a pretzel. It was large and brown with bright white specks of salt. And it was so soft. I was amused by the image. After that I began to think about food. I didn't care for the sandwich I made for myself today, as I rarely eat sandwiches. I examined my likes and dislikes regarding possible food suitable for a workshop lunch and decided that next time I will prepare rice and mixed vegetable curry to heat up in the microwave. I felt better having come to that decision. Then my mind went to thoughts about my body and I became acutely aware of my posture, especially my arms and legs. They felt quite solid and a little tight. I also became more aware of the sounds in the room, mostly the forced-air heater going on for a couple of minutes and then going off [I hope they fix that before the next sitting]. When the bell rang, I was quite present and relaxed.

Some Common Features of the Four Meditation Sittings

When I wrote the fictional accounts of these four meditators' sittings, I was aware that I wanted to acquaint you with some features that commonly occur in the Recollective Awareness approach to meditation. I will list these features and then explain them briefly for you.

- Uncertainty or confusion about what to do at times
- Fear or apprehension about getting caught up in certain thoughts
- Experiences of opening up to, or loosening around, the thoughts
- Strange experiences that arise from allowing thoughts to form
- Finding oneself in a calm state instead of trying to get calm

Uncertainty and Confusion

In the examples of meditation sittings that I gave, the meditators periodically remind themselves of the instructions. This helps them get oriented, but it helps only so much. In Becky's case (she was the first new meditator), she starts out reminding herself of one of the instructions: "Bring my attention to my hands, that's what he said." She does that instruction and finds herself thinking about Buddha statues and how the thumbs touch each other in the lap, which feels strange to her. Even though she does return her attention to the touch of the hands at another point in the sitting, this instruction is not being done as a task. She is not returning her attention to the touch of her hands throughout the sitting, so she has not turned it into something she should be doing all the time in meditation. Also, there is no specific goal in being with the touch of the hands—it is simply a place to which she can bring her attention. She doesn't know what she is doing yet, has no idea where the meditation practice leads, but that doesn't seem to bother her. Actually, she really doesn't feel uncertain about this form of meditation—she just doesn't know what to do at times.

The third meditator, Mark, has been doing two meditation practices side by side. This is not uncommon. When he does his mindfulness-of-breathing practice, the instructions and the task are quite clear: stay with the breath for as long as he can and bring his attention back to the breath when his mind wanders. When he practices Recollective Awareness, however, the question about what he should be doing comes up for him. It is not so clear to him. Should he bring his attention to his body? Should he let himself get caught up in thoughts? What should he do when he experiences a difficult emotion? In each situation that arises in his meditation sitting, he is faced with a choice to make regarding how to handle it. He is confused by not knowing what to do.

He is also uncertain about this kind of meditation practice. When he thinks, "I am still troubled by this whole notion of following your thoughts and not seeking pure experience," he is stating a strong and persistent doubt about meditating this way. But this moment of doubt doesn't get in the way. He continues to stay with his thoughts and emotions and begins to explore the nuances in the emotion he was feeling.

What I have found is that uncertainty and confusion are going to crop up in this form of meditation every so often, but they may not actually get in the way all that much. In my experience as a teacher, doubt about this practice can actually lead to serious reflections on meditation practice in general and can lead to understandings that would not come about if you were not allowed to question the principles and the purpose of this form of meditation.

FEAR AND APPREHENSION

The second new meditator, Jill, is seeking meditation to help with her anxiety. Sitting in meditation is bound to bring her into fearful and apprehensive states of mind. So, quite naturally, she would begin a meditation sitting with these kinds of thoughts: *I mustn't get anxious here, but I already feel anxious. How am I going to make it through this sitting? I can't just let my thoughts go all over the place for twenty minutes. I need to be able to rein in my thoughts. This just isn't for me.*

She needs a sense of stability, something that can give her a safe place to go to when she feels fear, and that is what the initial instruction of bringing her attention to her body sitting provides. She starts by bringing her attention to her feet, then her calves, and finally up to her trunk. She is not being guided to do this, and there is nothing of this sort in the instructions; instead, she discovers this "practice" on her own. And it seems to work, this time at least, to bring her attention to the sensation of anxiety in her chest, which then dissipates.

She sits for a while without anxiety, but her anxiety has not completely passed, as it returns later in the sitting. This is a more realistic scenario for experiencing anxiety in meditation. It comes back again, though it may not be about the same thing. In her case, it returns with thoughts about what to do and feelings of impatience, and it eventually brings her to think about a work situation that she is anxious about. But she is in a much better place to be having these anxious thoughts, more capable of tolerating the anxiety in them, and thinking more clearly about the situation.

There is another common scenario in this approach to meditation regarding fear and anxiety, and that occurs when a fearful thought arises of its own. This segment of Jessica's sitting illustrates what can happen: *She brings her attention back to her hands and is aware that she did that because she didn't want to go on thinking about her husband. She recognizes a little fear in her chest.*

"I really don't want to go into my relationship with Mark today. It is exhausting. And I have been avoiding it all week." The fear grows stronger, and she can feel it in her head. "I can't avoid it anymore. Here it is. I'm afraid we can't heal our wounds, repair the flaws in our relationship, that it is over."

She becomes more anxious after having allowed these thoughts.

One fearful thought, when allowed, can lead to another. That is quite natural. In this kind of meditation practice, however, allowing the fearful thoughts might also lead to a greater understanding of them. Sometimes when fear or apprehension first strike, it is hard to know what we are truly afraid of. It may take a few moments to register what it is. When she allows the thoughts to carry her away, she becomes aware of the kinds of actions she might take, such as leaving her husband, and is able to see how they are driven by fear and not by wisdom. Even though her fear of allowing fearful thoughts in meditation was realized, she was able to go through it and come out with knowing the fear in such a way as not to be deceived by it. The direction she went in was to probe more deeply into how she was seeing her situation, and her husband, and thus become aware of the more deeply rooted problems in their relationship. This, of course, may look like a psychotherapeutic process in meditation; the difference here is that she is doing it without external help, keeping her process private.

Experiences of Opening Up to Thoughts

The flip side of being afraid that thoughts will take over is the opening up to thoughts and trusting that you will not only survive them but also grow from the experience. After a meditation session is over and you reflect back on it, you may notice how little you controlled or manipulated your thoughts in the meditation sitting, and yet your mind quieted down and you became more aware of your thinking. It may strike you as odd how this happens, because almost every meditation instruction given to people promises they will reduce or eliminate thinking by putting their attention on something other than thoughts. While with Recollective Awareness, you have the effect of thinking less or thinking differently (in a good way) through opening up to the thoughts.

In each of the four meditation sittings, the meditators open up to their thoughts, but not without some reservation. Mark, for instance, takes a while to open up to his thoughts and does so only after he decides to allow his thinking to go on. And when he does become more allowing of his thoughts, he still has it in his mind as a ploy to get his mind to settle down. Only toward the end of his sitting does he seem to get some benefit from the thoughts he has and then feel some relief from thinking.

An important aspect of this process of opening up to thoughts is your resistance to doing it. What I have seen repeatedly is people who try to get past their resistance to thinking in meditation by telling themselves it is okay to think in meditation. That might help, but it goes only so far. You need to look at the thoughts that are telling you not to have thoughts. They are usually negative thoughts about thinking in meditation; they get you to think about controlling your thoughts, thinking different thoughts, stopping your thoughts. Let those thoughts go on and be kind to them. Then you are opening up to your negative thoughts about thinking in meditation, and your resistance will decrease. With thinking, you are always dealing with a moving, changing target.

Strange Experiences That Arise

Any meditation practice you do will most likely produce some strange experiences. In some forms of meditation, people are taught certain exercises, such as visualization, breathing techniques, body movement practices, or mantras, that will lead to particular kinds of meditative experiences. In Recollective Awareness meditation, as in mindfulness meditation practices in general, unusual experiences or altered states of mind are not sought after. They arise naturally as a consequence of sitting still and focusing on either the breath, bodily sensations, sense impressions, or by allowing your mind to go where it will.

When you allow your mind to have thoughts in meditation, you are also allowing your attention to move about freely. This free-ranging attention can sometimes lead to focusing on a part of your experience that has traditionally escaped much notice and thus set in motion a chain of events that culminate in some kind of strange meditative experience. When such experiences happen more naturally or, if you prefer, accidentally, then we often have no idea how or why they happened. One of the first things we may do after one such strange experience is try to figure out why it happened. This is often fruitless, but you may feel compelled to do it anyway. Instead of trying to find some reason or meaning for such experiences, in Recollective Awareness meditation we put our effort into recollecting these experiences and getting to know them better.

To illustrate this, I would like to use Becky's meditation sitting. She, as a newcomer to meditation, has no idea what can happen when she sits. Strange experiences are all the more surprising to her. As she is following the instruction of being aware of the touch of her hands as she sits, she pictures how she has seen a Buddha's thumbs touch each other. Later on in the meditation, she has the strange experience that her hands feel fused together, and then *a vivid image appears of two large white marble hands positioned like hers.* This progression of experiences is so unusual for her that she comments to herself about how strange meditation is and then considers opening her eyes to orient herself, but they seem fused shut. Another bizarre experience. But these experiences don't faze her all that much—she lets herself drift toward sleep and then goes to sleep, or into a sleep-like state, from which she emerges more relaxed.

Another type of strange experience commonly comes about from having a strong focus on something. A part of Jill's meditation sitting aptly illustrates this phenomenon.

She moves her attention up both of her legs and into her belly and chest, where she finds a vibrating sensation at the center of her chest.

"This feels like a knot. It also feels like breathing ice-cold air. But then at the center of it is a kind of buzzing, like there is a bee in my chest."

She focuses her attention like a laser beam on the buzzing sensation. It seems to get bigger, more diffuse, as if it were shaking apart as it grows. And poof! It's gone. Her whole body feels lighter, and there is less tension in her mind.

"That was strange! I wonder what happened. But I feel quite a bit calmer."

At first her attention moves up her body until it rests on a vibrating sensation in her chest. She goes into that sensation, eventually focusing on the center of it, and her attention is like a laser beam. In her case, this experience comes about receptively, without her actively seeking it, but there are meditation techniques that instruct people to focus on such sensations (usually painful physical sensations) and break them down into parts until they dissolve. In whatever way someone arrives at this experience of intense directed focus on a sensation, the result can be the dissolving of the sensation, which can lead to a type of euphoria.

A seemingly similar type of event can occur from noticing your thoughts, exploring them, and experiencing a bizarre representation (usually an image) of them arise. This doesn't come from the strongly focused attention of the previous example but, rather, out of a much looser process of holding a theme of the thoughts while thinking them. This type of experience cannot be made to happen intentionally, so it cannot be made into a technique. An example of this is from Jessica's meditation sitting.

Her attention moves of its own accord to her chest, where now she feels a tight knot but no fear. The knot is interesting to her, and she focuses on it. As she does, she starts to think: "I have been holding on to the habit of running away instead of facing things. It's just happening again. It seems to start with my avoiding something that has been bothering me. Then I finally try to face it and I get scared. When I'm afraid, I start to catastrophize and make frantic plans, as if the plans would prevent the catastrophe from happening. I've just begun to overthink it, but the first part is right."

She can feel the knot loosen. Her attention stays with the knot in her chest, and a vivid picture of a pretzel arises. She is startled by it.

"That is not the kind of knot I was thinking of. But it will do."

She does put her attention on the knot in her chest, but she doesn't hold it there, so there isn't the kind of strong focusing on the sensation found in Jill's sitting. Instead she allows her thoughts to lead her down a path that, in my mind, parallels the feeling and image of a knot in her chest. The feeling of the knot loosens as she gets more awareness of her thoughts and emotions, and when she stays with the knot, instead of vanishing, a strange image arises that represents it (a pretzel).

These kinds of experiences are just a fraction of the strange and unusual states of mind you can enter when you meditate. To illustrate many of the ones that occur in an open meditation practice would require much more space in this book than I am able to give it. Opening up to strange experiences is a prominent feature of an open meditation practice, and you may be struck by the variety of unusual experiences you have when meditating in this way. Most of them can be reflected back on and known more clearly. When doing that, we are not trying to find out what any of these experiences might mean. Instead, we are just becoming more familiar with them and, perhaps, discovering something about these experiences, or the states of mind, that we did not know before.

FINDING CALM STATES

There are so many meditation practices that are geared to relaxation. They try to get you to do something to relax your body and, generally speaking, empty your mind. This contributes to a situation where people feel that if they are not getting calm in meditation, then meditation is not working. They are failing at it. For some reason, their mind is not getting with the program to get calm. And if the calming meditation practice works once, why can't it work each and every time?

In Recollective Awareness we have a different approach to developing calm in meditation. It comes about on its own, when the conditions are right. Creating more tension or pressure to do a certain meditation technique in order to get calm in meditation will not produce the right conditions. But being more gentle with yourself in meditation, allowing your thoughts and emotions to be as they are, becoming patient with your mind and tolerant of the unpleasant things it brings up, and becoming interested in what is going on (not so driven to get somewhere) are all conditions that are conducive to calm in meditation. The only thing is, for a chunk of your meditation sitting, you may feel overwhelmed by your thoughts and emotions and be convinced that you will never get calm. It is a bit like going to bed and tossing and turning, thinking that you will never fall asleep, and then, without doing anything about it, you are fast asleep.

In this approach to meditation, people slip into calm states without any effort or intention to do so. It doesn't make any rational sense that allowing thoughts to go on in meditation will calm your mind, because that is not how it generally works outside of meditation. At first I didn't believe it. It took me years to finally come around to acknowledging that I was entering into calm states of mind more frequently, and more deeply, than when I was practicing awareness of breathing. One of my students, who had been meditating in more traditional ways before coming to me, recently remarked that allowing his thoughts at the beginning of a meditation sitting brought him more in touch with his body than starting the meditation with a body awareness practice. I know it doesn't make sense, but that doesn't stop it from happening.

In each of the fictional meditation sittings, the meditator finds herself or himself entering into a calm state, even if it is for a brief moment. The only meditator who seems to be actively seeking calmness is Mark. He believes his mind keeps taking him away from what is calm and still and that if he tries to keep his attention on the stillness of his body sitting, his mind will become calm. But that is not how it happens to him in this sitting. Instead he explores his sadness and lets himself think sad, hopeless thoughts and feel the pain of loss and failure. At some point in his anguish, he brings his attention back to his body, forgoing the technique of doing a body scan, and just lets himself stay with the sadness in his torso. And then, quite unexpectedly, where in one moment he felt very heavy and down, in the next, as if a knife had cut through the mood, he feels light and relaxed. This is a shift in his state of mind that I believe he could not have created by using a technique; with a technique, such as body scanning, he would have been so focused on the bodily sensations of feeling sad that he would not have "noticed" the thoughts and emotions connected with the sadness in his body. His experience of calmness would have been more like Jill's laser beam than like Jessica's pretzel.

That brings me to one last thing about calmness in meditation before I end this chapter. In Buddhist teachings, calmness and tranquillity are often associated with concentration. This leads to the notion that if you can get superbly focused on an object of meditation, such as the breath, then you will enter into a tranquil state. By equating tranquillity with one-pointed concentration, such practices have limited the ways in which people can become calm in meditation, setting up the situation that many meditators find themselves in, which is to keep bringing their attention back to the object of concentration whenever their mind strays from it. But as you can see from these examples, and hopefully in your own experience of meditation, your mind can become calm and tranquil without single-pointed concentration. In fact, it is the diffuseness of your attention, the way it opens up and allows your mind to go places, that often leads to calmness, peace, and, occasionally, sleepiness. In my previous book, *Unlearning Meditation,* I referred to this aspect of the process of calming the mind in an open meditation practice as "drifting off and waking up." It is perfectly normal, and in this approach to meditation, is one of the features of finding calm states of mind.

3

Talking about Meditation Sittings

Along with the notion that meditation is a solitary journey comes the belief that there is no point in talking about what happens when you meditate. Some people believe that since you can't really put your experiences into words, they are beyond language—there is no use talking about them. They may also assert that meditation is about getting past language and concepts and to direct experience, so it seems counter to that purpose to put words to what happens when one meditates. And along these lines, if meditation is about being in the present moment with immediate experience, then using words to describe it will take you out of the present moment and put you into the past or the future or, most likely, into the realm of concepts about experience instead of being in the experience.

It is true that we can't put our meditative experiences into adequate words much of the time, but that doesn't mean we shouldn't try. Words are a vehicle to recall, represent, and communicate experiences to others. They have limitations, but they help us get past other limitations that we face without them. For if we don't try to describe our experiences in meditation, what we are left with are supposedly nameless and empty experiences that are described as nameless and empty and left at that. The idea of not using language to describe, and eventually talk about, meditation experiences, where you're supposed to trust your nonconceptual understanding of your meditative world, can leave you in a place of not remembering much of what happens when you meditate and thus not learning as much as you could from your meditation practice.

This tendency *not* to put words to meditative experiences may not just be a matter of belief but may simply boil down to how much work and effort it actually takes to reflect back on your meditation sitting afterward and write it down so that you can talk about it. It is not easy to recall and articulate what goes on in meditation. You may need some help in this area. This is one of the main functions of the type of interviews I conduct with meditation students: to help them remember what went on during their meditation sittings. Writing down your meditation sittings is a good place to begin, but even then, some people find that they are just writing down the same old things for each sitting. This is where an interview with a teacher is most helpful.

The Interview Process

Let me give you a brief story of how this style of interviewing developed, and then I will go into more thoroughly.

When I was learning Vipassana meditation in Nepal, India, and Sri Lanka, meditation students talked about their meditation sittings only with a teacher. That was the custom, though it felt like a rule, one that had a good rationale behind it. Students were told not to share their meditation sittings with other students, and teachers made sure that they did not overhear each other's interviews. This was not done for privacy or confidentiality, as it would be in the West, but so that envy and comparison would not arise in the students. Since there were no personal questions being asked in these interviews, there would be little that a Western student would find needing safeguarding. What was feared had to do with students comparing notes on the instructions they were receiving, indicating to one another how advanced they were—it was believed that hearing about another student's experiences would bring about desire and envy.

Of course, an individual interview is done differently by different teachers and can have its own unique way of being conducted. Some teachers might just ask the same questions of every student. When they hear the "right" answers to certain questions, they ask some other questions, or they reach a conclusion about the student's experience and give the prescribed instruction. If the meditation practice has a particular instruction as its emphasis, then much of the questioning and dialogue will be about how the student is doing that particular instruction and what can be done to improve it if difficulties have been encountered. Such interviews might be done in ten to fifteen minutes—or be even shorter if the teacher has many students and little time.

Initially, my main modification to the traditional individual interview format was to lengthen the interview time to an hour so as to be able to hear more about the student's meditation practice. Instead of having a set of already formed questions to ask, I would ask the student to tell me what was going on in his meditation sittings. Most Asian-trained meditators were not used to relating their sittings in detail to another person, so I would occasionally have to ask questions about what they were experiencing at different points in the meditation sitting. Instead of my looking for something specific in their meditation sittings, which they were accustomed to having teachers do, I was helping them look at what was going on in their sittings. Sometimes I would go too far in this approach and try to get the student to describe each segment of his sitting in greater detail, which would create some tension in the interview, as no one can remember everything that goes on in a meditation sitting. So what I learned to do in these interviews was to gauge how the student was remembering things that occurred on the periphery of awareness and be satisfied with just a little additional detail. The way our ability to remember our experience may improve is by building upon what we recall easily and moving from there to what is harder to recall.

For example, a meditator may recall that she began the meditation sitting thinking about the meditation instructions and had some confusion about them. But then she can't remember anything after that. "It is all hazy." So I might ask her some questions about her experience before it got hazy. Does she recall her posture, any sounds in the room, her breath or bodily sensations? By answering these types of questions, she might recall aspects of her experience that are easier to remember. I might also ask her about her confusion. But whatever I do, I'm not going to immediately try to get a description of what it was like when all was hazy. That can wait. If a memory comes, it comes, but I'm not going to try to get her to remember something she can't. And after she tells me about hearing some sounds at the beginning of the sitting and noticing her breath slow down at some point and her body posture slumping a bit and her forgetting about being confused as she drifted into some kind of haze, then I can ask her a few simple questions about what it was like when it got all hazy. But these questions might not be what you expect. I might ask how long the hazy period lasted, when it ended, what it was like afterward. So I help build her memory of what happened before and after the period that she is having difficulty remembering. Then I might do something that sounds really contrary to my whole nonleading interview style. I could ask her if she felt floaty, spacious, serene; if she saw colors, lights, or images; or if she was aware of any thoughts or scenarios playing out in her mind. The reason I might feed her these kinds of descriptions, instead of asking her to describe things herself, is that I know how hard it is to remember what goes on in some of these meditative states and that giving a variety of possible experiences often jogs someone's memory. When she starts telling me that she saw colors and felt serene, then I can ask her about the colors and the kind of serenity she felt. Her hazy experience clears up just a little, but that is enough for her to develop greater familiarity with that meditative state of mind, so when she experiences something like it again, she may be a little more aware of it while it is occurring.

These are the kinds of interviews that new students are introduced to. As time goes on and I get to know the student better, the interview may go in a variety of unforeseen directions. But its baseline is always what you can remember from your meditation sitting, so even if the interview progresses into other areas of your meditation practice, such as your views about meditation or values regarding it, it always comes back to what happened in the sitting. In this way, the content of the interview, especially when it crosses over into the psychological and social aspects of your life, is firmly rooted in what happened in your meditation sitting and how you were with that content. So, for instance, if a meditator is thinking about her marriage, like Jessica in the preceding chapter, the interview could go into how she was with those thoughts in her meditation sitting and what she saw about herself from sitting with them, but it will never go into the area of counseling her about her marriage or asking intimate questions about her relationship.

The Interpersonal and the Group

Sitting in meditation, being silently still and inwardly focused, is an isolating activity. It brings you into contact with others as they appear in your thoughts. Your friends, fellow workers or students, partner, or dependents all enter into your meditation sitting as people you are thinking about or having imaginary or remembered conversations with, or whose presence you're feeling as some kind of physical/emotional memory of being with them. If you happen to do any psychological work on your relationships in meditation, you may find it to be one-sided, missing the input of the real other person. But that work on your side of the relationship may go further and be more honest and integral because you are doing it undisturbed in isolation. You are able to hold a situation (or an issue) in your mind for longer, and perhaps unpeel the layers and explore the intricacies of your complex inner world in ways that couldn't be done if you had to talk about it with someone.

Still, you will need to talk about things with people, as meditation will not work through everything for you. Meditation, of the sort I am describing in this book, will help you sit with interpersonal issues and explore them, but it won't fix them for you. That is something you have to do with the people involved. Just as self-honesty helps you go further into what is actually going on with you, honesty with others helps you go further in what is actually going on between you and other people.

Many meditators may question the value of talking about an issue with someone, because of having experienced a spontaneous letting go of certain issues in meditation. Some people may even hold the notion that since these issues have vanished, they really never had any substance—they weren't real somehow. What a shock when someone else brings up an issue you thought was dead, gone, or unreal! When that happens, are you prepared to engage the issue with the other person, or is that something you have grown out of or left behind?

Other people might go in the opposite direction and feel that everything they have discovered in meditation must be shared with another person, so that he or she will be able to be fully understood. Such discoveries might lead to confessions, to new and improved narratives, and to confronting behaviors that have not been working. Taking what you see about yourself in meditation seriously, and not just as passing phenomena, may actually have the effect of making you face up to things about yourself. But you don't need to tell everything you find out about yourself to someone else—you can keep what you are not ready to talk about private and share what you are comfortable saying.

We are looking at a middle way here, one that is between the extremes of full and exhaustive self-disclosure and the silence of believing all is done and buried. I, for one, tend to err on the side of silence, as I believe most meditators would. Meditation, being so much about finding calm and quiet, often attracts those who like to keep relationships calm and quiet. Meditation also attracts those who like to work on themselves in isolation, a do-it-yourself approach to psychological well-being, and so a fair percentage of practitioners prefer to do anything but talk about what they are thinking and feeling. So we need ways to move toward the middle way, by which I mean, find ways to have honest dialogues with other people about what is important in our relationships. One place to begin is in giving an honest report on what happens in your meditation sittings.

Group Reporting

I started offering people the opportunity to report their meditation sittings in groups at around the same time I was learning group psychotherapy. But I did not use the same format or methodology. It wasn't group therapy. It was group reporting.

In an individual interview session, the meditation student talks about her meditation sitting while the teacher asks questions and gives guidance. Group reporting is essentially an individual interview done in a group. For some meditation teachers, it is a quick and effective way to get updates on students' meditation sittings and can be particularly efficient when working with large numbers of students at a retreat. Such group interviews then may consist of the teacher asking each student a few questions and giving them instructions based on the replies. This type of interview might be satisfactory when teaching a meditation practice that relies heavily on giving instructions or tasks to do in meditation, but when it comes to an open, highly unstructured meditation practice, a different approach is called for. So I had to develop my own group interviewing format and style. Fortunately, I had worked this out in individual interviews, so the main area of learning lay in how to make it work in a group.

I will present a fictionalized version of a group reporting session on a residential meditation retreat. It doesn't matter whether it is a three-day retreat or a ten-day one; the reporting sessions are all done in the same way. What does matter is how many people are attending the retreat, how many groups there are in a day, and how many people are in each group. I try not to have more than eight people in a one-hour reporting group, but if I am teaching alone at a retreat of thirty or more people, I will up the number to twelve in a group. The most I can manage in a day is three groups.

Retreatants are not required to attend groups every day and can choose to attend only one or two groups if they like. Also, people are not permitted to sign up for more than one group in a day, but if they need an extra interview, they can always request an individual one.

At this particular retreat, with its twenty-four retreatants, eight people show up for my first group of the day. I recognize half of them as having attended previous retreats. The other four are new to me. I begin by giving everyone the group guidelines.

I say, "The way this is done is that one person will report at a time and everyone else will listen. The person reporting has as much time as she or he needs. You can talk about one sitting or a series of sittings. You may refer to your meditation journal when you talk. Please try to talk about your meditation experience in your own words without using any jargon. Be aware of your comfort level when sharing personal details. You can always decide not to share any details or go into more detail. Everything you say will be kept confidential. By confidential, I mean that you should not speak about anything anyone says in the group to anyone outside the group, and you should not talk to anyone in the group after the retreat is over (these are silent retreats) about anything that person or anyone else said in the group.

"Those of you who are listening will hear things that may be related to your own sittings. You don't have to follow the person's report all the way through. You can let yourself reflect on what you have heard. After each person is done reporting, there will be a period where you can ask me a question. Please don't ask any questions of the person reporting. We won't have time for everyone to report, and there is no pressure to report.

"Who would like to begin?" I ask the group, looking at each face, knowing that it often takes a minute or two before someone speaks up.

Usually new people don't report first, so I anticipate one of the others, and as I look around, I see that Penny is preparing to speak. Penny is in her sixties, a psychologist from Brooklyn. This is the third retreat she has attended in the past three years.

She says, "I want to talk about this morning's meditation. The two sittings last night were difficult, since I was feeling that I really didn't want to be here. I have done this retreat each year for the past few years and thought I should do this one too, but as soon as I got in the car and drove here, I was filled with doubt. I didn't sleep well either. But this morning's sit was better. Is it all right if I read it?"

"Certainly, go ahead," I say.

"Birds chirping. I'm not used to hearing so many birds. I don't know what kind of birds they were, but some were very shrill and loud. Then I remember thinking about M, who after five years still has the same anxieties, the same addictions, and the same loneliness. It made me think about whether I am a good therapist. 'Not all of my clients are like this,'" she says in an aside, looking up from her notebook in her lap, her face red and moist from tears. She returns her attention to her journal and picks up where she left off. "I was feeling down about myself, but it was bearable. I went through one client after another, seeing if I had failed them, and saw that I hadn't. Many have improved." She looks up again and smiles to everyone in the room.

"I don't know how it happened," she says, "but I must have forgotten about my sadness completely, as I was feeling very calm and light. Then I noticed the birds again. There was one with a lovely song." She tries to imitate the sound but botches it, and a couple of people in the group laugh—not in a mean way; an uncomfortable laugh, it seems.

Penny looks a bit more self-conscious and resumes reading from her journal with her head down. "I was able to follow each note. When I came to the end of a passage of the bird's song, I suddenly felt quite still and calm. It was a second of profound peace. The rest of the sitting was very peaceful, and I knew why I had to come on this retreat." She shuts her book and looks right at me.

There are a few places in Penny's report that I could begin with. I consider what she is interested in looking at in this sitting. It sounded as though she went through her feelings of inadequacy and failure at the beginning of the sitting, and I wouldn't want to start the interview by focusing on something painful. I might start by asking her about the experience of feeling down about herself becoming more tolerable as that relates directly to how she is developing greater tolerance for certain emotions in meditation. But still, that is beginning the interview with something painful—I don't have a rule against that but prefer to extend a courtesy to the meditator by not setting the tone of the interview in the direction of emotional pain, especially when the person has gone through the pain in the sitting. I would rather foster trust in the meditative process for helping her through the pain than dig it up again in the interview. She has moved through it for now. If it comes back during the retreat, then we may look at it. I don't want to set up issues for students to look at in their sittings but want, rather, to leave them to explore what it is that is coming up for them receptively.

I remark, "After you thought about one client after another and saw that they had improved, you said that you don't remember how it happened, but you seemed to have dropped your sadness and moved on to feeling calm and light."

"Yes," Penny says, "that was a bit unexpected. I thought the sadness would last longer, especially since it has in the past. But usually I would believe my feelings of failure and inadequacy. Here I questioned them. Not because it was a good idea or someone told me to but because those feelings seemed suspicious to me at the time.

"Then I was able to see one person after another whom I had helped in the past. It was a bit like doing a loving-kindness type of meditation, thinking of one person and then another, having a kind and warm feeling about each one, but it wasn't contrived. Maybe it was the feeling of being kind to others, and then to myself, that helped me move away from my sadness and become lighter."

"That could be," I say. "Has that happened before?"

"Yes, it seems to be the way my meditations go these days. I have periods of regret and sadness, and then it opens up more."

"When it opens up more, like it did in this sitting, do you become more aware of other things, like the bird sounds you mentioned?"

"Yes. Sometimes it is the breath or my body, but this time it was sounds."

"Do you recall what it was like after you followed each note of the bird's song? What that part of the sitting was like?"

"I don't remember much besides being very calm. . . . I might have been aware of the birds for a while, and then it seems like I drifted. I felt like I was sunk in my body. I wasn't asleep, but I wasn't entirely alert to what was going on around me. It was a different kind of feeling."

"Did you notice any colors or light?"

Penny pauses to reflect, and I can see that she is going back over that period of her sitting.

As we wait for her to respond, let me tell you something about this interview. It has been my experience that when a student reports a calm state that lasts a while in the sitting, it is likely that not much of what went on has made it into memory. The student may need some help remembering what went on. So my questions may then supply the person with possible "objects of awareness" that might appear in a calm state. Colors and light might be something that was there that the person did not remember all that well.

She replies, "I do recall that at some point there was a grayish expanse. I know it was there because it was pitch black before. It wasn't bright. It was like concrete after it has rained. That was all I saw."

"Then what about internal sounds or thoughts?"

"Very few thoughts," she says. "They just seemed to float by. But each time I thought something, it seemed so clear at the time, though I forget it all now."

"Did that last until the bell rang at the end of the sitting?"

"The bell brought me out. It sounded far away. I could feel it reverberate; my body seemed to vibrate with it. I came back slowly and opened my eyes. My first thought was that this is what I have come here for."

"Well, good, we'll stop here," I say.

While I wait for the next person to report, let me fill you in about how this interview progressed. It may seem to you that not much happened. There wasn't any great insight, there were no major issues or themes uncovered, and even the calm state may seem unremarkable. That is the way many interviews go. They are not meant to end on a high note. The purpose of such interviews is to expand one's awareness into areas of one's meditation sitting that are normally not remembered and therefore never known or examined. So I began by asking her about how she moved from feeling sad to feeling calm and light, which was a transition that she had no real memory of. In responding to my question, she mentions how she was suspicious of feelings of inadequacy and so didn't believe them as she would normally. This exploration of those feelings and the subsequent release from them happened on its own, not requiring her to do anything in particular. When she reviewed the clients that she has helped in psychotherapy, she recalled having a warm feeling about each one of them, as though she were doing a loving-kindness meditation practice. This too happened without intention and it felt genuine.

By my going into the calm state she experienced, she will now be more familiar with that state and most likely will have better recall of it. And I know, from my years of teaching in this way, that she will experience this type of calm state on more occasions, and it will become a feature of her practice. In fact, it already has. One thing that I gleaned from her report was that she has turned this state into something she wants to have again in meditation. It may even have become the reason for coming on this retreat. So instead of being a rigid Buddhist meditation teacher and trying to get her to see the desire and clinging she has for this calm state, I am more practical. I want her to keep meditating and experiencing wholesome states of mind, so I approve of her experience, even though she seems attached to it. When she starts reporting that she is craving that particular state, then we will talk about desire and attachment. But, for now, it is working for her. That is why I ended the interview where I did.

The next person to report is a newcomer. She is an attractive woman probably in her early thirties. I know that her name is Alice, as I had memorized everyone's name the previous night. I have no idea about her meditation history, her background, or anything about her, since we didn't have intake forms on this retreat.

"I didn't write much about my sittings, and I don't remember much, but I have a question," Alice says.

"What is your question?"

"I get this feeling when I meditate that my body is very big. It expands."

"That's a fairly common experience," I say.

"What does it mean?"

"I don't interpret experiences for people," I reply. "Has it happened in your sittings here?"

"No, it hasn't," Alice says. "I haven't felt that calm and focused yet. It usually takes three days for my mind to settle in a retreat."

I have to pause before I respond, as her last comment communicated quite a bit to me, and now I have to process it. I have heard from many students that they expect their mind to settle down on the third day because they have been on retreats with teachers who have told them that. Why can't people be left alone to experience their mind settling down in their own time? Okay. So she has been on meditation retreats before, probably ones where she was instructed to stay with the breath and return to it when her mind wandered. She has probably heard many talks on the right kind of effort and discipline to bring to meditation practice and is carrying those notions with her as she hears my instructions to the students to do the practice they have been doing, or not do it. She probably likes the instruction to be gentle to herself. I am now ready to hear what she is going to report.

"Well, do you remember anything about this morning's sitting?" I ask, knowing that for most meditators the morning sitting is what they consider their best time to meditate.

"Yes," she says, "it was okay."

Alice doesn't seem to want to talk about her meditation practice in the group. This happens on occasion. Someone wants to ask a question, get an answer, and then say nothing. I don't usually pursue the person beyond asking two or three questions. I'll ask another question and then move to the next person if she doesn't want to say anything.

"You came to the meditation hall and sat on your bench, an hour passed; is there anything about that period of time you can talk about?"

"Well, I couldn't get comfortable on my bench," she says. "I tried to bring my attention to my breath at the abdomen but couldn't stay with it. I kept falling asleep." She looks ashamed of this as she says it. That's probably why she didn't want to report. I regret having her say something that brings up shame for her, but how was I to know? Now that I do, I can maybe help her feel okay about falling asleep in her meditation sitting, if it was sleep that she was going into. "It's all right to fall asleep here."

"But what if I snore?" she asks, and then looks around the group and adds, "I don't want to disturb people in the hall."

"Were you snoring this morning?"

"I don't think so. I mean, I wasn't fast asleep. It was more like dozing and waking up."

"Did you have any dreams?"

"I would pop in and out of dreams. They weren't like ordinary dreams. I would hear two people having a conversation, but I don't know what about."

"Would you just hear the conversation or would it also be a bit like a movie scene?"

"Yeah, once or twice it was like a scene from a movie. I can almost remember one of them. There was a little girl holding her mother's hand and looking up at her. What she said was nonsense, but the mother said, 'Be still now.' I remember that clearly because I then thought about being still and wondered if I was being still or not. When I was still, I wasn't doing anything. That is what I came to . . . I'm so glad I have that memory."

"That's good. We'll end here," I say.

Now Alice is smiling, and I can see that she has a better feeling about her experience this morning. I pause a moment before moving on to the next person, a young man named Richard who has been to several of my workshops over the last few years. When he came to me, he expressed concern about his fear and anxiety, since he has had many anxiety attacks and wasn't sure he would be able to meditate if he suddenly got anxious.

Richard begins his report by saying, "There really wasn't much happening in my morning meditation, but then something interesting happened. I was thinking about being away from my wife and son while on this retreat. There was guilt at first, and then I felt some fear about something happening to them while I'm away. I sat with these anxious thoughts and allowed myself to feel the fear in them. I observed my body and was aware of sadness in my throat, a vague impulse to cry, fear in my stomach, and my whole body as a lump of pain.

"After a bit I heard myself say 'I don't like that.' The intention to let go surfaced. My mind released its hold on the pain, and then my body relaxed. As my mind became more spacious, my throat and stomach became less tense, my whole body became less tense, and my mind became more free and I became more and more peaceful, without any thoughts."

I pause for a few seconds before asking him, "When you had these anxious thoughts of something happening to your wife and son while you were away at retreat, did you bring your attention immediately to your body?"

"Not immediately, no," Richard says, "I became aware that my thinking was a bit paranoid, which sometimes happens, and when it does, I tend to pick up on an underlying mood of fear in them."

Richard has heard me talk of looking at the underlying mood in the thinking as a way to see what may be driving the thoughts in the present moment. So he picked up the fear in the thoughts, and that brought him to awareness of how the fear was manifesting in his body.

So I ask him, "When you noticed the fear in your body, did that change your experience of the thoughts?"

"Yes, the thoughts seemed to go away and leave me with this fear in my stomach. As I focused on my stomach, sadness erupted in my throat, and for some unknown reason I felt like crying." His faces reddens for a moment as if to cry, but he doesn't.

"Were you able to cry?" I ask.

"No, it was just an impulse to cry; no tears came."

"You didn't try to figure out why you were sad?"

"No, it didn't seem fruitful to go there. Instead I noticed how my whole body was covered by this kind of pain, which was like being in a hot bath when the water is too hot. I stayed there, as I would in a hot bath, waiting for the water to cool down and become pleasant, but it never did, and I told myself I didn't like the pain. . . . Well, not exactly. I actually recognized that I was creating the pain and my mind could just let go of it if it was willing to, and it did."

"What I hear you say is that you had an understanding that your mind was creating the pain, not your body, and that led to a letting go of it."

"Yes, that is how it happened."

"Were you in a calmer, more focused state of mind when that happened?"

"Yes, I was considerably calmer then. It was as though the calmness I was experiencing with the pain broke the pain apart and moved into the foreground of my experience. The tension in my body kept lessening, and my mind was getting spacious."

"By spacious you mean . . . ?"

"No thoughts, nothing to hang on to, in a pleasant way."

"We'll stop here," I say.

After a series of interviews, I often take questions from the people in the group. They must direct all of their questions to me and cannot ask questions of each other. This often leads to discussions about different types of meditative experiences.

Alice, who was the woman new to this approach to meditation and the second person to report, asks, "When you were talking with that fellow," she points at Richard sitting across from her, "he said something about 'underlying moods.' I didn't get what he meant."

"What he is referring to," I say, "is how our thoughts may have an underlying mood or attitude in them. We might not notice it as a bodily sensation, though sometimes we can feel it. Mostly, however, we can get a sense that there is a pervasive mood that underlies our thoughts." I stop for a moment and try to think of an example and then go on, "It is like when you are planning on taking a vacation, not that ordinary trip you take to see relatives or parents, but one of those big, exciting trips to a foreign country. You might notice that as you are thinking of the places you will be staying and the sights you will see there, there is excitement in the thoughts. When you think of getting visas, going through customs, the possibility of your baggage getting lost, then there may be some dread or apprehension underlying the thinking. And when you think of getting to your hotel room and lying down and resting after a long day of sightseeing, you might find there is a kind of relaxing mood in the thoughts, a sense of relief."

"What do you do to bring your attention to this underlying mood?" She asks.

"At first you might not pick it up," I reply. "You may be thinking for a few minutes and then realize that there is a mood operating in the background. It will usually surface into awareness of its own, but you may have a habit of pushing it away. There is no need to hunt for it. But also, you might pick up some clues by noticing the tone of voice in your thoughts and the attitude in the thinking."

"Thank you," she says.

The next person to report was a woman by the name of Karen. This is her first retreat with me. She has mostly done traditional Insight meditation retreats and was intrigued by this approach from reading an article of mine.

"The theme today was 'How did I get here?' I kept noticing how I'd be present, set an intention to see what was occurring, and the next time I was aware was when I *came to* in a particular thought. I could feel how the mind latches on to thoughts. Today it seemed to be localized in the left eye and left side of the head. It was astonishing and annoying that I didn't have any control. I was interested in the mechanism that kept taking me away but couldn't identify it."

Since Karen expressed interest in the mechanism that kept taking her away from what she intended to focus on, I asked, "You knew how it felt when your mind latched on to thoughts and where it was localized in your head; is there anything else you can remember from being in your thoughts?"

"No, not really," Karen replies.

"Were these mostly pleasant thoughts?" I then ask.

"They had to do with future plans and were more practical than anything else."

"Like you had to get something done, and yet here you were sitting in meditation, not able to do anything?"

"Yes, like that. My mind just wanted to figure things out so that I would be prepared."

"And yet you wanted your mind to settle down and be present?"

"Yes, that is it."

"So what was creating the conflict was not your mind pursuing future plans but your intention to be present, which I take to mean to be with your breath, bodily sensations, or sounds."

"But isn't that what I am supposed to do in meditation?" Karen asks, truly surprised that I am questioning the practice of returning one's attention to the present moment.

"Well," I say, "it sounds like that is what you have done in your previous meditation practice and continue to feel a need to do in this one. . . ." I pause to reflect a moment before pursuing this subject further. "The area of investigation here might *not* be to look into the mechanism of your mind going into the thoughts but, rather, the way your previous meditation practice of returning to the breath has interrupted your thoughts. Of course you are not in control of these thoughts in the sense that you can't just turn them off at will. They need to be allowed into the sitting."

"So what you are saying," she says, "is that I should look at the mechanism of stopping my thoughts rather the mechanism of lapsing into thought."

"Yes."

"That's interesting," she says.

"And much more doable," I reply. That ends this interview.

I pause for a minute before asking the whole group if they have any questions.

Alan, who is a newcomer to this approach as well and didn't report in the group (since reporting is not mandatory, not everybody does it), has a question. He is probably in his thirties and his facial features express some irritation, which I assume has to do with what he has heard me say.

Alan asks, "That whole interview with that woman over there seemed upside down and just plain wrong."

"What are you referring to?" I ask.

"Your advice to look at the mechanism of stopping thoughts rather than the mechanism of being carried by thoughts." He pauses and looks around to gauge people's expressions, notably mine, hesitant about saying more. Alan then says, "Isn't learning how to stop thoughts a good thing? That is what we do in meditation. We stop thinking and go into quiet states of mind."

"Yes, in one respect, you are quite right," I say. "Thinking can slow down or stop, leading to quiet states of mind. But how can that happen naturally, without forcing it? That is what I am trying to help people get to."

Still not satisfied, he asks, "Well, how does it happen naturally?"

"What I have heard in the reports of many meditators is that by allowing their thinking to go on in meditation, it reaches a point where it either exhausts itself, and their mind calms down, or they see something about how the thinking is fueled, and through that insight, the thoughts die down and vanish. But this can happen only through the allowing of thoughts in meditation. If you stop your thoughts all the time, then there is no possibility that you will gain insight into what fuels them."

"That is enough for today. We'll stop here," I say to the group.

4

Six Common Ways to Become
Aware of Thoughts

When practicing an unstructured approach to meditation, there
are periods when, in the midst of not knowing what to do, one
will try out a structured approach. I don't see any problem in doing this, as long as it is done experimentally and not religiously,
and the act of doing it does not require force or aggression. So
some meditators do experiment with other ways of becoming
aware of thoughts in meditation, and these are often intentional
practices that people have heard about. To my knowledge, there
are essentially six common ways of becoming aware of thoughts,
emotions, and mental states found in modern-day meditation
practices. There are probably more, but the following six cover
enough of the territory to be useful.

1. *Noting* or labeling
2. *Witnessing* or observing
3. *Tracing back* a train of thought
4. *Focusing on* a thought or emotion
5. *Analyzing* thoughts and emotions
6. *Inquiring into* a thought or emotion by asking questions about it

I will talk about each of these intentional practices (techniques) in relation to practicing Recollective Awareness meditation, where, on occasion, one of these practices may be done unintentionally, arising out of the meditative process.

Noting

A meditator will often ask me about noting his thoughts and feelings at times when he has difficulty remembering his experience. This kind of noting is like leaving breadcrumbs that can be recovered at the end of the sitting and used for recalling what went on. Sometimes it is done more actively as a way to stay awake and alert during periods of drifting toward sleep. Other times it is seen as a remedy for not being aware enough when in a tranquil state where there isn't much going on. The need to be alert and conscious, knowing what is going on, is often behind the implementation of labeling one's experiences in this approach to meditation. Rarely is noting done for the reasons it is taught in the Mahasi method of Vipassana meditation (to be mindful of each moment; see chapter 6), and if a meditator experiments with present-moment noting, he generally experiences the force and aggression in that practice, which goes against his orientation to be kind and gentle with his mind in meditation, so it doesn't take hold as a formal practice. It is just an experiment.

The main consequence of noting your thoughts and emotions in meditation is that the act of noticing them individually will interrupt your thought process and thereby hinder any further attempts to get to know your thoughts and emotions as they would function naturally. The noting itself is a new thought about what it is you are thinking and can lead to a running commentary on your experience. This may in turn lead to identifying with an observing knower. That knower is thinking thoughts about what is going on and is taken as an authority on one's experience, yet the thoughts, emotions, biases, values, and beliefs of the knower are never scrutinized. What develops out of this practice is a privileged "knower of the field" who is never called into question; in fact, a witnessing consciousness is often seen as stable, pure, unaffected, detached, and endowed with higher knowledge, so questioning its assertions and judgments is unheard of.

Witnessing

When a meditator comes to me with questions around becoming aware of thoughts and emotions through detaching from them and witnessing them from an equanimous vantage point, I often have to tread lightly. Being such a clear witness to your experience feels like you have arrived at the optimal way of practicing mindfulness. With that optimal observing consciousness, you can notice your emotions without getting caught up in them; you can see your thoughts pass by like clouds across a clear blue sky; and you can dwell in a still, peaceful state of mind for periods of time. What exactly is the problem here?

There are actually several issues with this equanimous observing state of mind, but none of them are apparent when you are in such a state. When in it, everything is perfect, or nearly so. When out of it, ordinary ways of being may be seen as unsatisfactory or, at the very most, bearable. This detached witness becomes the true way of being, the essence of the mind, or enlightenment. A need forms to get back into that specific state of mind. Meditation is then construed as the way to get into that state and stay there longer. Your ordinary thoughts and emotions, and perhaps even your relationships with others, are considered mundane and trivial in comparison. Being in that state of mind all of the time, merging with it, seems like the only true way to enlightenment, awakening, liberation, peace, what many sages through history have all spoken of as the highest, unsurpassable consciousness. But is it?

A detached observing consciousness is a mental construction, meaning that it is a subjective state of mind that is created. It too arises and passes away. Sometime later it rearises and goes away again. What seems to give it objective permanence is the belief that it exists all the time somewhere. But in truth, it is just like our more mundane and ordinary thoughts and emotions. Just as we go through an hour or two of getting angry about some slight or other, we go through a period of time of being a nonjudgmental and unaffected witness of our experience. Where do our thoughts and emotions go when they vanish? We probably don't say that they exist for eternity somewhere. But when a higher observing consciousness vanishes, many who believe in such a consciousness as an objective reality probably see it as residing somewhere. What the Buddha was asking people to consider is that states of consciousness do not reside anywhere; they just come about when the conditions are right.

It occurs to me as I write this that there is a "feeling" of being detached and knowing one's thoughts as they appear, and this feeling is quite convincing. It is like the feeling of a self or a soul, or the feeling of the presence of God. One cannot use logic (or quote research) to counter the power these feelings have over us. The situation is essentially, "When I am a detached observer, it feels so true and real, I cannot believe that my mind may have created it."

Getting back to the practical side of observing thoughts, creating an observer or witness to your thoughts may help you identify certain thoughts that you cannot see because you are so embedded in them. In that respect, the practice is similar to pausing a moment and reflecting back on what you had just thought about. Except the distance from the thought seems to occur in the moment instead of after the fact. Please consider that the in-the-moment distance is actually still a reflecting back on the thought, though in a shorter than normal time span.

Tracing Back

This brings me to the topic of tracing your thoughts back to some kind of origin or trigger. An origin is usually that point of initial contact out of which a whole train of thoughts arose. It is usually conceived of as either a "pure" state of mind that is yet unsullied by thoughts, such as bare sense perception, or the place from which thoughts rose into existence. Tracing back your thoughts to this origin becomes an exercise in finding the source of thoughts, not in trying to understand the sequence of thoughts. With either of these two views in mind (the belief in a pure unmediated sense experience or the moment of a thought's arising from emptiness), your investigation into the nature of thoughts is slanted toward identifying experiences that are prior to thoughts and thus void of them. These are not practices that lead to a greater awareness of thinking but, rather, an attempt to transcend thought by seeing its origins in something that is not thought.

The more modern psychological notion of finding the trigger to a train of thoughts usually involves a recollection of each thought as it occurred until you find yourself at the inception point. This is a practice of becoming aware of thinking after the fact, much like Recollective Awareness meditation. The difference, however, is that when you trace your thoughts back to their trigger, the method is one of seeing how one thought led to another. Usually these thoughts are moving from one to another by virtue of associations being made, as in this example: *I was meditating during my weekly sitting group and I heard someone cough. I immediately wondered how close I was sitting to that person. Then I wondered who it was. By the sound of the cough, it was a man. The man I pictured was a middle-aged man who has been coming to the group who reminds me of my brother. My brother's face came into my meditation, and he looked sad. I thought about how I have disappointed him, but then I corrected myself and saw more clearly that I have been disappointed by him.*

If the meditator traced back her thoughts right then, she could easily pick up one association after another: identifying the cough as belonging to a man, picturing the man as someone in the group, seeing the resemblance between that man and her brother, having an image appear of her brother's sad face, and finally thinking about having disappointed him and realizing that it has been the other way around. So what began with someone coughing during the silent group meditation led to her contemplating her relationship with her brother. Tracing back the sequence of thoughts in this case, and many like it, just gives you some idea of how you got to thinking about something, but it doesn't offer much insight. In this example, the act of tracing back to the trigger of the thought took the meditator away from what I believe is really of value in her experience—correcting her perception of having disappointed her brother to seeing how he has disappointed her. This is a richer and more meaningful area to explore than trying to find out how she got there, and in the process of doing an exercise of tracing her thoughts back, she could miss out on being with thoughts and emotions from which she can learn.

In Recollective Awareness meditation, the looking back over thoughts during a sitting can be a way to notice a thought or emotion that you passed by too quickly. This may happen more frequently with thoughts and emotions you are not comfortable with, where they appear as a blip on the screen. So you may need to recall those feelings you passed over. But in doing so, you may not be able to go into them. It is enough at this point just to acknowledge that you felt shame, dread, lust, hatred, envy, or whatever kind of emotion it is normally hard for you to stay with. In time, you may be able to be with such feelings longer, and you may be able to tolerate them more and become interested in knowing them more intimately.

Focusing on Thoughts and Emotions

This brings me to the fourth item on the list, which has to do with consciously focusing on a thought or emotion and following where it leads. There are two extremes that people fall into when doing this in meditation. One is focusing on the emotion and making stories out of it. Someone who does this would most likely be aware of an emotion—for instance, a feeling of dread—and get the dread to dialogue with him or her, treating the emotion as a person with its own history, consciousness, and will. The other extreme is to view the emotion as a bodily sensation without any story attached to it. Then the pure sensation can be focused on, and eventually the sensation will dissipate or dissolve. Both of these approaches require holding the thought or emotion in the mind (and body) and staying with a process either of story making or of concentrating on the bare sensation.

When focusing is done in the extreme of concentrating on the bodily experience of an emotion, it generally divorces itself from looking at how thoughts and emotions interact. The effort is on staying with the physical manifestation of an emotion, and any thoughts that enter are most likely distractions from doing that. Such practices tend to divide thoughts from emotions (or feelings) and may even rationalize the split by saying that the thoughts are in the emotions and sensations, and thus can be successfully worked through in the body without ever needing to be aware of them in the mind.

In Recollective Awareness meditation this kind of concentration on sensations is not recommended, though it can occur quite naturally from time to time, and when it does, it is fine for however long it lasts. For the most part, however, this approach involves mending any of the splits between mind and body that may have occurred in one's life and/or previous meditation practice. So the direction is not to focus too strongly on any physical sensations but, rather, to allow thoughts and sensations to mingle and affect each other. In this way you will see more of how thoughts and emotions condition physical sensations and how your bodily experience conditions your mental world.

The practice of focusing on an emotion and creating new stories can lead to greater awareness of the history of an emotion, where it fits in your relationships, what it might mean when you feel that way, and how the emotion might support certain behaviors, among other things. The new stories may be built on old ones, or they may be novel creations.

Focusing on the old stories that come up is something most meditators are warned against and, besides that, are naturally disinclined to do. The rationale is that if you spend too much time with your personal stories, they will just keep running. And if you get hijacked by these stories, you will end up believing them. But I don't see this particular scenario playing out all that often, so I have come to doubt its validity, seeing it more as a myth about meditation rather than a fact.

Analyzing

What tends to happen, especially with people who have either been in talk therapy or done some work in that vein, is that the person starts to analyze her thoughts and feelings. This kind of analysis often takes the form of asking questions about why you are thinking these thoughts, what they say about you, where they come from. Sometimes the analysis goes in the direction of discerning the exact qualities of the thought and emotion, such as whether a feeling is of rage, hatred, spite, or contempt. This kind of discerning of emotions is one that I believe is more in tune with Buddhist practices of developing a discerning awareness, which is aided by the use of synonyms and is something I will explain in the next chapter.

When the analyzing goes in the direction of speculating about why you have certain thoughts or feel the way you do, then it may feel less like meditating and more like psychotherapy. But I would suggest that you let such analyzing go on and see where it goes. Sometimes it might bring you closer to a memory or emotion you have been avoiding. Other times it might spin off into a contemplation of certain views and values you hold. And then again, it might lead you to some self-knowledge that is new and other knowledge that is old and questionable. There are many directions in which your analysis of your meditation experience can go—the question here is twofold: Are you directing the analysis to some predetermined conclusion? Or are you allowing the analysis to unfold more naturally, occasionally moving from those thoughts to check back in with your experience of sitting in meditation?

It may sound as though I am advocating analyzing your thoughts and emotions in meditation, but what I am really putting forward here is a particular kind of analytic thinking that is found in what I call an explorative process. This kind of thinking is actually not speculative, in that it is based on what you know at that moment about your experience. So if someone is meditating with a childhood memory of, say, being rocked in her mother's arms, the exploration is about how one is feeling at the moment sitting with that memory, what kinds of thoughts and images that memory evokes, and how one understands some of the causes and conditions surrounding that memory. Such memories may confront certain old stories she has held on to about her mother and may cast her mother in a more caring light. To then analyze her relationship with her mother, as would be done in psychoanalysis and other forms of analytic psychology, could take away from the impact of the memory and the simple exploration that is unfolding. In those schools of psychotherapy, when practiced by skilled clinicians, there is usually more information gathering, more inner searching on the analysand's part, before the therapist offers an interpretation. The holding back of any interpretation in those forms of therapy may be done so as not to stall a potentially fruitful investigation into difficult and complex psychological issues. In the types of exploration that may arise in an open meditation practice, any premature interpretation not only may conclude the exploration just as it's getting started, but will also most likely generate superficial ideas about why things are the way they are, instead of the more profound kind of insight that can arise from a gentle and patient process of exploration.

Inquiring

When someone is given prescribed questions (such as "Who am I?" or "What is this?") to take into her meditation sitting, the practice may not lead to an awareness of thoughts, for many ordinary thoughts will be passed over in favor of those that pertain to the question. Such questions may actually serve the similar function of an object of concentration, such as the breath, where the idea becomes to stay with the question, even if an answer is not forthcoming or is not part of the practice, as holding a thought (which is what a question is) in your mind to focus on can produce concentration.

There is a difference when the questions arise more naturally from what you are experiencing. These questions may not have a prescribed flavor to them. They may be more specific to what you are thinking, feeling, remembering, or intending at the time. There may be curiosity and interest behind the question. And such questions will most likely be in your own words and pertain to what is presently going on in your meditation sitting.

These questions occur after the fact and often accompany a recollection of something that you just thought about or felt. Rather than looking at this as something to do purposely in meditation, it is more appropriate to attune yourself to such questioning as it naturally occurs. If you treat your questioning thoughts as thinking that is distracting or getting in the way, then you may not let them lead to an exploration of your experience. What we are looking for here is a way to have relevant questions about what is going on in our mind when we meditate, and those questions have to relate to what we are specifically experiencing and not to some general notion of what we should be seeking to understand. Instead of asking "Who am I?" or "What is this?" why not listen to the questions that naturally emerge when you reflect back on your experiences?

Sometimes these will come up as questions, while at other times they may arise as doubts, confusion, or just feeling that you don't know what is going on. It might go something like this: *This state of mind I am in seems a bit sleepy, but then again, I am awake in it. I have been calling it dozing for some time now, but that doesn't seem to describe it. It is a little too bright and buoyant to be dozing, though I feel heavy in it. What is this heaviness? It has a smooth, fluid quality to it and draws me toward sleep, or at least I think it is sleep. Maybe it isn't a precursor to sleep like I always thought, since I don't fall asleep in meditation when I feel this heaviness.*

This simple kind of inquiry, which is just questioning how you have been describing a particular experience, allows your experiences to be more open to investigation and to be reconsidered in a different light. Without this kind of periodic inquiry into how you are describing particular experiences to yourself and others, you may find that you continually talk about experiences in the same way and don't get beyond those initial habitual descriptions. And it can be surprising how much can change in the course of your meditation practice by simply questioning a word or phrase you have been using for certain experiences and see where that leads you.

Asking questions or being in doubt about a state of mind in meditation is of course different from dealing with the great questions of life. Sometimes we think we need to bring these larger questions of existence into our meditation sittings instead of just letting them arise naturally, as if we won't ever consider them unless we intend to. But such questions can come up when just sitting with your ordinary thoughts and feelings, though they may not seem so profound at the time. Let me give you an example from someone's meditation journal:

Sick of my mind. Spent the sit giving myself permission to slow down, bringing in patience, letting go. Just thoughts about how sick of the mind I am and of the self and the petty stuff I get steamed up about and then dreamy stuff, coming back every now and then to the hands in the lap or sitting. I saw that it is useless trying to anticipate anything at all, that the self is all puffed up feeling so important—as if anyone would care that I spent the weekend mostly alone??? I was trying to deal with the suffering I give myself—that no one loves me, no one invites me, I'm alone; trying to make myself see that it is fine, I DON'T HAVE TO ACHIEVE anything, do anything to be able to justify existence—see the fear of having no importance, my life being of no importance, and then thinking I have to prove something, but I don't really. . . . That is all part of constructing an identity. What if I proved nothing all day? It's like looking into a gaping void of not being important, but all the time was the sense that just beyond the veil of all of this, there is real nonsuffering—that is, being comfortable with not being important and doing nothing of importance. I can almost see it, almost know it.

The way this person's meditation sitting starts off with being sick of her mind, you would not think that she would come to *the sense that just beyond the veil of all of this, there is real nonsuffering.* She follows the themes her mind brings up about her life, and though she is not inquiring in any directed or intentional way, she both feels and at the same time questions her need to justify her existence, to prove something, to use her time productively. In the course of those thoughts and feelings, she can inquire into the need to construct an identity around her experience and find that she can almost see herself being comfortable with not being important, not doing anything important—and in that may lie her freedom from suffering.

Using These Six Ways of Being Aware of Thoughts

When any of these six approaches to being aware of thoughts is applied in a directed or formulaic manner, they may not only control one's thoughts in meditation (by creating a predetermined focus of attention) but also create a model of how thinking operates. Observing one's thoughts from a distance, for instance, will create a model of the thoughts' being somehow separate from the observing consciousness. Tracing back thoughts to their origins will lead to a model of thoughts being linear and, for many people, to a belief that if they could just get back to the moment before the thoughts began, there would be no thinking, just pure witnessing or perceiving. For those who have practiced directed inquiry into thoughts and emotions, there may be a belief that when the right questions are asked, it is only a matter of time for the right answers to come. All of these models or formulas may appear valid for some people at certain times, but they each carry a partial notion, which is often made into a global one, of how thinking works in meditation. In my opinion, none of these ways alone leads to a more comprehensive and accurate understanding of thinking in meditation.

But when each of these common ways of being aware of thoughts arises naturally in an open meditation practice, where they are used as temporary ways to look at thoughts and better understand them, then they each may fill in gaps that would be found in using just one of these ways. In my discussions with other meditation teachers over the years, I have learned that many of them have found that just observing one's experience is not enough. There needs to be some kind of inquiry as well. And inquiring isn't sufficient either, so sometimes engaging the student's memory and ability to reflect on experiences, ideas, and actions is called for. With all of this information gleaned from observing, tracing back, and inquiring, there may need to be some way to analyze, to sort through and integrate these experiences and understandings. So by not cutting off any of the available ways to become more aware of the inner workings of our mind, we find what is suitable at this point in time, follow it, and see what comes of it. In my experience, both as a meditator and as a teacher, that has been most useful.

5

Meeting Your Thoughts at a Resting Place

There is a particular Buddhist discourse titled *Vitakkasanthana Sutta* that is taught as the Buddha's way of working with thoughts in meditation. When I teach in a more traditional or orthodox setting, I encounter people who swear by it and take me to task on it. So, with this chapter, I am going to face my biggest critic, the Buddha himself, as he is interpreted by scholars and lay meditation teachers alike. When this discourse is viewed with unprejudiced eyes regarding thinking in meditation, one may find that the Buddha may actually be saying something closer to what I have been saying all along: get to know your thoughts in meditation, but be careful how you handle unwholesome thoughts.

To begin with, each translator of this discourse makes his bias known in how he translates the title. Soma Thera shows his antipathy toward thoughts by choosing to name his translation of the *sutta* *The Removal of Distracting Thoughts,* while Thanissaro Bhikkhu offers an unbiased literal translation for his version: *The Relaxation of Thoughts.* Just from the title alone, if someone read Soma Thera's translation, the person would be inclined to look for ways to remove distracting thoughts that get in the way of meditating on a particular meditation object. But even this does not support the notion that all thinking should be eliminated in meditation. According to Soma Thera's translation, "the evil unskillful thoughts are eliminated; they disappear." The emphasis in the discourse is thus not about eliminating all types of thinking but only "evil unskillful thoughts" that are connected with "desire, hatred, and delusion." Unfortunately, a view that all of our thinking is connected with desire, hatred, and delusion has crept in and muddied this picture for certain Buddhist meditation practitioners, so, for them, the broad stroke of eliminating all thoughts seems to be in order.

Venerable Thanissaro's translation of the Pali word *santhana* as "relaxation" is much closer to one of the original meanings of the word, which refers to a "resting place, a meeting place, a public place (market)." This notion of a resting place as a place where one stops at the end of a journey probably gave rise to a secondary, more abstract meaning of "stopping" or "ceasing" when the word *santhana* is applied to thoughts. Surely in the minds of those who seek a pure mind that is absolutely free of thoughts, the Buddha could not be talking about "meeting your thoughts at a resting place." But what if that is exactly what he meant to those who first listened to him? The Buddha speaks in this discourse about "resting with" (though people have tended to see this discourse more as "wrestling with") all kinds of thoughts and what to do when unwholesome and unskillful ones catch hold of you.

This way of resting with thoughts is found in the first instruction on what to do with thinking. The Buddha is careful to say that it is not a passive affair, where one would allow unwholesome and unskillful thoughts to lead one completely astray, but I believe he also does not say that it is an active one either, where the meditator replaces unwholesome thoughts with more wholesome ones, such as practicing loving-kindness at the first sign of an angry thought. It is somewhere in the middle, and yet, like many things in the middle way, it is entirely different from either extreme.

I will make reference Venerable Thanissaro's translation throughout this chapter, as his title, *The Relaxation of Thoughts,* best captures a middle-way orientation to being with thoughts in meditation. His wording of the *sutta* passages is more complicated than Soma Thera's translation (Bhikkhu Bodhi's translation is greatly indebted to Soma Thera's and uses the same title) and will require a bit more concentration on your part, and work on my part, to get at what is being said.

After the initial statement about where this discourse takes place, the Buddha gives an introductory overview of what he will cover in this day's talk:

"When a monk is intent on the heightened mind, there are five themes he should attend to at the appropriate times. Which five?"

Before I continue presenting the Buddha's discourse: there is some confusion created in this discourse by the Pali word *nimitta,* which Thanissaro translates as "theme" (Bhikkhu Bodhi translates it more traditionally as "sign" and Soma Thera, in this instance, translates it as "thing," and later on as "object"). It would be clearer to translate the last part of the preceding passage as "there are five strategies he should employ at the appropriate time." This makes the most sense, as the Buddha goes on to describe one strategy after another for dealing with recurring and pernicious unwholesome thoughts, basically saying that when one strategy fails, here is what you should do next.

After this opening statement, there is an assumption regarding the meditator's practice that needs to be clarified: "There is the case where evil, unskillful thoughts—imbued with desire, aversion, or delusion—arise in a monk while he is referring to and attending to a particular theme." I believe the assumption here is that the meditator is attending either to the breath; to a prescribed contemplation; to a loving-kindness practice; or, more in keeping with the language of this discourse, to a *jhana* practice of staying with a particular image, light, color, perception (*nimitta*), and so forth. The unwholesome thoughts are coming up and taking his attention away from concentrating on his prescribed object of meditation. It would then follow that each of the five strategies is designed to bring his attention back to his primary object of meditation, so that "he steadies his mind right within, settles it, unifies it, and concentrates it." Without a doubt in my mind, this discourse is referring to *samatha* practice rather than *vipassana* meditation. Its direction leads to tranquillity (*samatha*), and the procedures are essentially done in the service of settling, unifying, and concentrating the mind, which are the key features of a *samatha* practice.

This whole discourse may not really be applicable to an open awareness meditation practice, such as Recollective Awareness meditation. And if it is applicable to an open, highly unstructured meditation practice, then it relates to the processes by which a meditator divests himself of unwholesome and unskillful thoughts and arrives at settled, calm states of mind, even without relying on a primary object of meditation. So from now on in writing about this discourse, rather than perceiving it as a critique of an unstructured approach to meditation, we can view it as mostly speaking to a practice of concentrating on a primary object of meditation, with some relevance regarding what happens when we do allow thoughts and emotions, especially the negative variety, into our meditation sittings. So instead of taking it as prescriptive, I would like to look at these strategies as descriptive of what you may find yourself doing in meditation in regard to thinking.

In Thanissaro's words, the first strategy goes something like this: "If evil, unskillful thoughts—imbued with desire, aversion, or delusion—arise in a monk while he is referring to and attending to a particular theme, he should attend to another theme, apart from that one, connected with what is skillful." The strategy here is to bring your attention to a different theme from the meditation object you are using. This would traditionally be interpreted as a practice of replacing unwholesome thoughts with wholesome ones. So if you are focusing on the breath and have some persistent angry thoughts, then the instruction is to bring your attention to another theme, such as loving-kindness. You would then intentionally practice loving-kindness meditation until "those evil, unskillful thoughts—imbued with desire, aversion, or delusion—are abandoned and subside. With their abandoning, he steadies his mind right within, settles it, unifies it, and concentrates it." When those

unskillful thoughts subside, your mind becomes settled and focused, which quite naturally happens when you divest your mind
of troublesome thoughts, inner conflict, and emotional turmoil. In
this particular *sutta,* there is no instruction regarding what to do
when your mind is thus settled and concentrated, but the assumption is that you could return to the original theme of the meditation
sitting, which in this case would probably be awareness of the
breath.

In an open meditation practice like Recollective Awareness, a
similar procedure of shifting your attention to a skillful "theme"
when sitting with persistent and intense unskillful thoughts would
eventually occur. But it won't happen by deciding what the new
theme will be. Instead, it comes about by noticing the skillful or
wholesome states of mind that are already present while you are
thinking unskillful thoughts. So while you have thoughts of
disliking somebody on account of something he said, you may also
be aware that there is some compassion for yourself for the unkind
feelings you are having or some interest in why you are thinking
those unkind thoughts or perhaps a sense of the suffering involved
in entertaining such thoughts and their possible actions or any such
skillful theme that is also present. These skillful themes will arise on
their own—there is no need to insert them into your meditation or
try to create them at the first instance of feeling angry or upset. If
you can be patient and tolerant of your experience, they should
arise, though they may be subtle and hard to notice at first. And
often when there is a shift from the persistent, unskillful thought
process to the more skillful one, you may notice a settling down of
your mind and a growing calmness. But you may be aware of this
transition only after you have been free of the persistent thoughts
for a while. Sometimes the calm state that follows has a sleep-like
quality to it, so that you might not easily recall how you shifted from
feeling angry and upset at someone to being calm and drifting.

Now, if this first strategy doesn't work, the Buddha recommends
a second strategy: "He should scrutinize the drawbacks of those
thoughts: 'Truly, these thoughts of mine are unskillful, these
thoughts of mine are blameworthy, these thoughts of mine result

in stress.'" It seems to me that the Buddha is recommending shifting your attention from a primary object, such as the breath, to looking carefully into the thoughts you are having that are particularly unskillful. He is not advocating this strategy for all thoughts but for those that are truly "dangerous" (*adinavo*, which Thanissaro translates more neutrally as "drawbacks"). To me, dangerous thoughts are those that are undeniably unskillful, which inevitably lead to regrettable words and deeds and will only end up creating more stress or suffering. Experientially, when having such thoughts, there may be no ability to be kind, interested, or patient. This is not an ordinary situation, where you could possibly summon up some good skillful quality of mind. It is one where you are swept up in something dangerous, such as a sexual fantasy that involves cheating on a partner or engaging in sex with an inappropriate person. What is recommended here, I believe, is meeting these thoughts and resting with them in a way that allows you to look at them squarely and see their consequences. Only through such scrutiny will they subside. It may take a while, and you might not be successful. . . .

In that context, there is the third strategy: "He should pay no mind and pay no attention to those thoughts." This is an interesting suggestion at this point in the process, whereas, if this strategy had been given at the beginning, people could just say that the Buddha first recommends paying no attention to unskillful thoughts. But he doesn't. He recommends withdrawing attention from those thoughts only after one has looked deeply into them, having examined them and seen clearly the danger in them, and not before. It is fairly common in Recollective Awareness meditation for someone to sit with unskillful thoughts for several sittings in a row, tolerating them and having periods of exploring them as well as some short breaks from them. Then it becomes possible to decide not to get involved in them anymore, and they fade away. I believe it is this kind of process that the Buddha may actually be referring to here: disentangling from powerful and persistent unskillful thoughts may come after having met them appropriately with skillful qualities and investigating them.

But what if they keep cropping up again when you have with-drawn your attention from them at this point in the process? That is where this fourth strategy comes in: "He should attend to the relaxing of thought-fabrication with regard to those thoughts." What follows as a description of relaxing the thought-fabrication is this: "Just as the thought would occur to a man walking quickly, 'Why am I walking quickly? Why don't I walk slowly?' So he walks slowly. The thought occurs to him, 'Why am I walking slowly? Why don't I stand?' So he stands. The thought occurs to him, 'Why am I standing? Why don't I sit down?' So he sits down. The thought oc-curs to him, 'Why am I sitting? Why don't I lie down?' So he lies down. In this way, giving up the grosser posture, he takes up the more refined one." Though it sounds simple, I think this is actually a bit confusing, so I will try to explain what I construe the Buddha to mean here.

My sense here is that the person should direct her attention to the speed, rhythm, or tone of her thoughts. So it is not "thought-fabrication" that is relaxed but, rather, the active process of think-ing those thoughts. Instead of exploring what one is thinking about, explore the voice that is speaking the thoughts. This voice has a speech rhythm, a tone or attitude, and will remind you of somebody else or of yourself at certain times. Putting your atten-tion on these aspects of the unskillful thoughts can have the effect of gradually slowing them down until they stop altogether. The idea that lying down is a refined posture would be the case only if it is a metaphor for the mind's becoming settled and still.

Now, if that doesn't work, the Buddha seems to recommend a very extreme last resort: "With his teeth clenched and his tongue pressed against the roof of his mouth—he should beat down, con-strain, and crush his mind with his awareness." The simile for this action is also a bit drastic and out of place for a paragon of peace and compassion. It reads, "Just as a strong man, seizing a weaker man by the head or the throat or the shoulders, would beat him down, constrain, and crush him; in the same way . . ."

I hope your experience of meditating with unskillful thoughts never gets to the point where this seems like a sane and practical approach. If it does, remember that the Buddha is saying "crush his mind with his awareness" and not with self-hatred, shame, or any self-destructive or aggressive thought. I would like to think that the Buddha is suggesting that you be so aware of the unskillful, unwholesome, dangerous, and despicable thoughts, staring them right in face, that they are beaten down, constrained, crushed.

The end of this discourse has something relevant to say about this whole process of meeting your thoughts in meditation and enabling them to relax. For when one has done this, it is said: "He is then called a monk with mastery over the ways of thought sequences. He thinks whatever thought he wants to, and doesn't think whatever thought he doesn't. He has severed craving, thrown off the fetters, and—through the right penetration of conceit—has made an end of suffering and stress."

What the Satipatthana Sutta Says about Thinking

The Four Satipatthanas, more commonly translated as the "Four Foundations of Mindfulness," form the basis for much Vipassana meditation practice and teaching. The four foundations are (1) *kayanupassana* (the body), (2) *vedananupassana* (feeling tone), (3) *cittanupassana* (mental states and thoughts), and (4) *dhammanupassana* (mental phenomena). The word *anupassana* means "looking at, contemplating," or "recollection" and is the method for developing mindfulness of each of these four arenas of our experience.

Since I can't cover each of the four foundations in this chapter, I have decided to concentrate on the third foundation of mindfulness, that of mental states and thoughts. Most every Vipassana method introduces the meditation student to the first foundation of mindfulness, usually through the practice of mindfulness of breathing, and then may have the student include awareness of sensations, feelings, thoughts, and mental phenomena. In Recollective Awareness meditation, the beginning instructions include awareness of the body (the first foundation) as a place to return your attention when needed, but that is used only to help you stay with your thoughts and emotions (the third foundation). The other two foundations of mindfulness come into one's awareness as well, but once again, they are not practiced using any prescribed technique. You are simply aware of the feeling tone of your experience and the various mental phenomena.

You might wonder why I don't see Recollective Awareness meditation as beginning with the fourth foundation of mindfulness, that of mental phenomena. The reason for this is simple. When people begin meditating in a predominately unstructured practice, the last thing a teacher like me would want to do is teach them a whole new set of terms and give them models into which to fit their experiences. That is essentially what would be required if I taught the fourth foundation of mindfulness. I would have to instruct students to notice the five hindrances; to see their experiences as made up of the five aggregates and not-self; to be alert at the six sense doors; and, as their practice progressed, to become familiar with the seven factors of awakening. This would not be a practice of Recollective Awareness meditation but, rather, a practice of learning how to see your meditation experience in terms of the Dhamma. Over the years, I have been leaning toward the translation of *dhamma*, in the compound word *dhammanupassana* (the fourth foundation), to mean "seeing the teachings on the Dhamma in your experience" rather than "looking at mental phenomena."

The third foundation of mindfulness is actually quite simple, with no new terms to use. We are used to talking about angry thoughts, desirous thoughts, and deluded thoughts. We may each have our own word preferences, but no one needs to be taught a whole set of new terms and difficult concepts before embarking on the project of self-awareness in meditation. You already know enough to begin. Just as in the first foundation of mindfulness, where it takes no additional learning to bring your attention to your breath, you are equipped to become more aware of your thoughts from the outset.

Bhikkhu Analayo, in his book *Satipatthana: The Direct Path to Realization,* states that the method for the third foundation of mindfulness involves being receptive to one's thoughts and emotions. He writes, "It is noteworthy that contemplation of the mind does not involve active measures to oppose unwholesome states of mind (such as lust or anger). Rather the task of mindfulness is to remain receptively aware by clearly recognizing the state of mind that underlies a particular train of thoughts or reactions." The only area of possible disagreement I have with this statement (or confusion you might have about it as you read on) is that I do believe awareness of the content of your thoughts is as important as being aware of the process: clearly recognizing the state of mind that underlies a particular train of thought does not occur by disregarding the train of thought in favor of seeking an underlying process that one believes is the truth, or essence, of thought.

The Pali word for the third foundation of mindfulness is *cittanupassana*. *Citta* is actually not a very easy concept to translate into English. It takes from such concepts as consciousness, mind, heart, cognition, and intentionality, but is not reducible to any of these. "States of mind" or "mental states" seems to work the best for the Theravadin interpretation of the word. Mental states have their own thought processes, moods, emotions, and ways that we are identified with them. By looking at thoughts and emotions, we are looking at mental states. When we identify ourselves with a particular mood or intention, we are taking up a mental state as a self, such as when we feel sad and hopeless, we may identify ourselves as being depressed. When we believe that the mood and thoughts we are experiencing is a self, we may see it less as a temporary mental state that depends on conditions and more as a fixed and stable self that resists change and improvement. One of the main purposes in practicing awareness of mental states is to look at the changing states of mind we go through and see how we identify with them, while we also learn how to see them as made up of conditions.

As I have been saying in regard to Recollective Awareness meditation practice, looking at thinking is done by recollecting thoughts rather than trying to be in the present moment with them. Mental states have duration. When you are in a particular mental state, it will last for a period of time, and many times you have no idea how long that will be. You may fear that getting angry at someone for a few minutes will lead to hours or days of feeling awful about it or that you may go through a lifetime of unnecessary bitterness and resentment toward that person. But you may find that you feel awful for only a few minutes afterward and any residual feeling stemming from your episode of anger might not solidify into a grudge. You would know that only after the period of anger had subsided and was replaced by other mental states. While you were angry, you would have little idea of how it was going to play out unless you had recollected such experiences on several occasions and explored the conditions that arose and supported the angry mood.

In the Buddha's choice of words for states of mind, he is offering six distinct vantage points from which to view thoughts, emotions, and states of consciousness.

- With lust, anger, or delusion: discerning conditions for mental suffering
- Focused and conflicted thinking: discerning conditions for concentration or exploration
- Higher states and lower states: assessing states of mind
- Surpassable states and unsurpassable states: questioning attainments and realizations
- Tranquil states and not so tranquil states: discernment necessary for developing tranquillity
- Liberated (or freed) states and bound states: discernment necessary for nonattachment

Categorizing Mind States

I do *not* believe that there is a mind state of greed or desire that underlies a thought process of desiring. What underlies a thought process of desiring is a complex web of conditions that are suited to the person's psyche and character, not a mind state of desire that has its own existence.

There is a particular translation issue in this section of the Satipatthana that deserves mention in this regard. When referring to awareness of desire, the *sutta* says, "One knows a mind with desire as 'a mind with desire.'" This wording is often interpreted to mean that the Buddha is talking about a "mind of desire," which is often understood to mean that the mind is entirely composed of desire and there are no other qualities present (because of the view that only one mind state arises at a time). If you look into your thoughts as containing desire but not entirely or purely made up of desire, then you might notice that there are other qualities or emotions as well. The same holds with anger and delusion, the two other unwholesome states of mind mentioned in this discourse.

The Buddha could be talking about the words we use for mind states, not the mind states themselves (for there actually are no pure mind states of lust, anger, and delusion). As such, the Buddha could be saying, "When you are aware of a mind state with desire, know it as 'a mind with desire.'" In this way, the Buddha would be helping people direct their attention to their experience in a very simple manner, where they become aware of thinking about wanting something and call that experience desire. It is then just a practice of being honest with yourself about what you are thinking and feeling. Then such terms as *desire, anger,* and *delusion* would not be mental states but, rather, words that people use to talk about their experiences. This is how most people untrained in Buddhist teachings would look at the situation. Thus the Buddha is simply telling us to notice desire, anger, and delusion when they arise by naming them and admitting their reality to ourselves.

Such a practice will go only so far. On the downside, it may just lead to lumping a great variety of experiences together under one heading and noticing them in a perfunctory, automatic way. It can also produce a distance from your emotions, even though at first it may seem like a way to manage them when they get too strong. Generally speaking, labeling desire, anger, and delusion in one's meditation sittings may be helpful for a period of time, but soon enough it loses its freshness.

DOSA—ANGER

I have found that the most useful and interesting way to use this language in meditation practice is to hold the label as provisional and discern more closely what the experience may be more like. For instance, starting with a feeling that gets labeled as anger, you may notice that it is more like resentment than anger. This finer discernment through language may lead to a greater connection with the experience and therefore to a more thorough understanding of it. You may go through a few synonyms for anger before finding one that fits. In this way, the label of "anger" branches out into the various words that would get subsumed under anger but are distinctly different shades of the experience. So instead of trying to bunch together a range of anger-like feelings under that single term, the direction is to find the words that best describe the feeling. In looking for such words, while staying with the feeling, you are exploring the experience, going further into it in order to understand it better. This is the opposite direction of stepping back and labeling the experience as anger and then trying to manage it or moving on to something else.

So, how would I suggest you use this section on "looking at, around, and under" your greed, hatred, and delusion? Instead of reducing your experiences to fit into these three categories, I would recommend noticing the specific details of your experience. What might strike you as some angry thoughts at first can be looked into further to reveal more detail. It would be like taking a magnifying glass to a cut gemstone to see past the surface faceting and into the interior of the stone. You may call it anger, but inside the experience it has its own structure, its own unique contours, its own history and provenance. It may feel the same as other angry moments, but you know that it has unique things about it. I suggest looking at those unique features instead of lumping the feeling into one more instance of being angry and trying to move past it.

An example of such an exploration within a meditation sitting might look something like this: *I keep calling this feeling anger when it comes up, but I am not so sure about it anymore. There is a familiar tension in my chest and limbs, and a scalding sensation across my shoulders and the back of my head that I associate with anger. But my thoughts are more resentful than angry, leaning more toward hurt and betrayal than actually being angry. If I let go of the tension, I could possibly sink into some sadness, which I feel a bit on the edges. When I touch the hurt, one impulse after another arises, telling me I must do something about this—he who hurt me has to pay for this. These impulses are anger, but the general mood I'm in is not an-*

gry. It is more nebulous. I don't have a name for it, though it is familiar, but not exactly the same as something I have experienced before. There is an enveloping mild calm state, which is like two hands holding a living bird, whose rapidly throbbing heart and fluttering wings are like those impulses.

In this type of contemplation, there is no labeling of the experience as "anger." It is initially identified as a kind of anger, but it is not seen as definitely anger and nothing else. Instead, the naming of the experience as anger is questioned in a way that aids in looking at the other details of the experience, such as the other thoughts and emotions that were also present. There is no speculation about the experience—no questions as to why this is happening or what it means or where it comes from. The meditator in the example stayed with how the experience was unfolding and did not try to figure it out or direct it in any deliberate or prescribed manner. The progression toward the end was one of expanding out from the core emotional experience (anger, hurt, sadness) to how it was held (in a calm state of mind). So not only was the experience of anger gone into with more detail, the mental environment that it was connected to was also explored and known more fully.

Moha—Delusion

One of the main problems with using the concept of the Pali word *moha* is that when translated exclusively as "delusion," it is used to cover all of our mental experience. We can get a clearer, more circumscribed picture of what *moha* probably refers to when we look at it as referring to foolish, childish thoughts and emotions. These thoughts and emotions could be distinguished from anger or desire. A foolish way of behaving, such as joking around or friendly teasing (as entertaining as it might be to oneself), is neither an angry way of being nor a particularly lustful way. When joking around or teasing, you might say some childish or foolish things that might seem cruel, but they are not said out of anger. You might also poke and tickle but without any sexual feeling. Your intention may be to get the other person to laugh or lighten up, and the only way that comes to mind is to act the fool. This, I believe, is one aspect of *moha*.

Another kind of thinking is dull, forgetful, or drugged thinking.

Your mind is just not operating up to par and you tend to say things that are mistaken, not factual, unclear, or more deluded than usual. This kind of *moha* may also incline you toward lethargy, apathy, sleepiness, and futility.

Delusional thinking is well worth noticing, just as much as angry or greedy thoughts, but the problem most people have with such thoughts is that they may seem sane and reasonable at the time. Looking at your few minutes of paranoia when you think someone is speaking ill of you when she isn't may be hard to do in the present, as you are paranoid and not asking that kind of question, but it may be more possible after the fact. We just hope our paranoid moments are truly short-lived so that we can wake up from them and reflect back on them.

Present-moment awareness may also be largely unavailable during other deluded states of mind, such as psychotic breaks or breaks with reality. If a person wholeheartedly believes in a delusion such as "I am an alien and not really a human being," bringing present-moment awareness to the situation may be used only to confirm the delusion. The same type of scenario occurs with some of the delusions that can accompany severe depression. No matter how you try to convince the depressed individual that his life is worthwhile and he is a good person and capable of living a healthy life, he may be able to be aware of only the thoughts and feelings of being worthless and a bad person, and the hopelessness of having a better life. When the person moves out of the depression and some of the deluded self-assessments, there may be a chance to look back at the episode of delusion.

What I am saying here is that while present-moment mindfulness of the thinking may not be possible, or if it is, it may fail to bring with it a desired sanity and reality-testing to disconfirm the delusion, reflecting back on the experience is entirely possible. The reflecting back on any kind of delusional thought process, and exploring it from a more reliable state of mind, may actually provide insight into it.

RAGA—DESIRE

As with *moha* (delusion), if the mental state of *raga* (lust, desire) is seen as a feature of practically all mental states, then there is no impetus to discern what *raga* really is. The Buddha's choice of the word *raga* in this context is important. He was referring to lust for enjoyment, for possessions, for a better self (more beautiful, wealthy, successful, famous), for what would seemingly make one happy in the material world. *Raga* is not used for desire for peaceful states of mind or liberation from suffering. It is focused on acquisition and enjoyment in the world of the senses.

Before I say more about *raga,* I must ask you not to give in to some kind of moralistic guilt about being a slave to your desires. That won't help you to meditate with this mind state. I have heard many meditators over the years express their guilt over having sexual fantasies in their meditation sittings, as if their minds should be free of such thoughts when they meditate. Actually, the opposite may be true. Your mind is likely to have more such thoughts during periods of boredom, restlessness, and discomfort. When a meditation sitting isn't providing you with the kind of calmness and clarity you are looking for, you might find that thinking about sense pleasures is an easy substitute. Or you might find that when you sit down to meditate, all you can think about is sex, food, entertainment, intoxication, and obtaining more possessions. Instead of pushing that out of the meditation sitting, let it stay. Since you are meditating with the intent to be with and contemplate the mental state of sense desire and not to act on it, you will not be feeding the fire in the same way as you would in a situation where you were actively entertaining yourself with a fantasy. When you take up the task to understand how desires for sense pleasures work, you might find that meditation is a good laboratory to conduct your explorations.

Other kinds of sense desires may appear trivial and not worthy of serious attention while you are meditating, so you may tend to disregard or ignore them. A shopping list starts to form in your thinking and you stop it after a couple of items with the idea that meditation is not a suitable place for you to think about your shopping. Something that you have been yearning to buy occupies your thoughts for a while and you put it aside because you are not going to decide on that purchase while you are meditating. A movie you want to see comes to mind and you note it for viewing later but have no interest in looking at why you want to see it. And this final instance in this list of disavowed desires: you start thinking about a person you would like to spend more time with, and even without sexual overtones, you opt not to pursue such thoughts in your meditation sitting, thinking, "What good would that do me?" In these situations you may believe that you are restraining your mind from pursuing fantasies based on desires and that you are thereby not fueling desires, but what you may be doing is developing apathy and avoiding actually dealing with your desires.

Many of our desires run our lives because they are never examined. Noticing that you have a desire and bringing your attention back to the breath is not examining desires—it is not even a practice that is conducive to the possibility of exploring how desires come to be and what keeps them alive. And such meditation practices assume that the meditator is fully onboard for the eradication of all desires somewhere down the track. They don't even bother to ask you where you honestly stand with your desires before giving you a practice and philosophy geared to put an end to desires someday. No wonder this whole area of desires is so confusing for so many meditators.

The complexity of your desires for sense pleasures is what can make investigating them very interesting. If it were as simple as seeing a photo of an attractive person of the sex you are attracted to and then you become attracted to that image and seek out that person in your fantasies and real life, all you would have to do is stop seeing photos of people you could be attracted to (which would be difficult given the modern-day pervasiveness of such images). The Buddhist monastic notion of restraint would work for you. Then if it were a simple case of looking at autopsy photos of similarly attractive people, who now have become repulsive, and then you begin to feel repulsion for human bodies, whereby you supposedly lose your lust, then the monkish practice of contemplating the foulness of the flesh has worked for you. You may think that it is a bit weird that I bring this up here, but such contemplation is a part of the first foundation of mindfulness (that of the body), in a section on contemplating the uncleanness of the body. And several monks I knew in my time as a monk shared autopsy photos among themselves as a modern way to do this practice.

Since most of you will not go the route mentioned above to root out sexual desire, which frankly, I don't believe has done much rooting out for those who practice it, you may need to take a more civilized and complex path of seeing what all of these sexual, sensual, and pleasurable thoughts are about. Knowing that no one is fully 100 percent behind eliminating all sense pleasure, that you have a lifetime to spend on this planet and still have things you want to experience and enjoy, even if it is just your daily routine of small pleasures, I will continue with this exploration of sense pleasures in a manner that I think you will be more comfortable with.

In order to meditate and develop awareness regarding sense desires, you don't need to stop a desire altogether; you may just need to exhibit occasional restraint. With intoxicants and addictive drugs, you may need to go through some program to quit them, as meditation may not lead to giving them up. But it would be advisable not to use intoxicants before you meditate. People have asked me about whether they can have caffeine before a meditation sitting, and it seems to be up to how the person is affected by drinking it, so I suggest if you are concerned about being too wired during a sitting, then don't have any caffeinated tea or coffee.

By occasional restraint, I mean that if you tend to watch a few hours of television a night, you might just watch one hour a night instead of not watching any. If you spend a few hours a day shopping on the Internet, perhaps it would be good to shop for a few hours only every so often. If you have a love of chocolate, you might want to limit your consumption. If there is no action taken on limiting or cutting down or spending less time pursuing sense pleasures, then you may not feel as though you are seriously looking at them. Also, the limiting of such desires means that these desires may enter into your meditation sittings more readily, as you may now be using some of the time you have gained from limiting your desires to meditate.

So, to be clear, I am not asking you to cut out anything from your lifestyle. I am only asking you to exercise some restraint and set limits for your desires. If those restraints and limits become problematic and get in the way of your taking time to meditate, then you can decide what to do about it. The last thing I want is a situation of deprivation followed by a period of bingeing.

FOCUSED AND CONFLICTED THINKING

Moving on from the three poisons (greed, hatred, and delusion), the discourse then presents a pair of words that are ambiguous at best. The words are *sankhitta* and *vikkhitta*. *Sankhitta* means "concise, brief, or contracted" while *vikkhitta* means "agitated." The commentaries relate these terms to two hindrances: laziness and restlessness. This is presumably done so that there is a tight correlation between hindrances (found in the fourth foundation) and the first five mind states listed in the third foundation. This correlation of mind states to hindrances is a bit stretched. The terms used for each of the five hindrances are different from the ones used for the first five mental states found in this *sutta*. On the basis of that alone, any strict correlation between the two is a matter of interpretation. So, having rejected what the commentaries teach on this matter, I am left with exploring what *contracted* and *agitated* might mean.

It becomes easy to turn these two terms into something very abstract and neat, as they beckon one to make a mental model with them. I'll show you what I mean. They can be opposites: contracted/expanded, focused/scattered, concentrated/agitated, concise/voluminous, brief/long-lasting. You can choose any of these pairs as a way of noticing your thoughts and the states of mind in meditation. And though they may be of use, no one interpretation is right, because we really can't know what was actually meant by these words said in this context by the Buddha.

They are just not mentioned often enough, nor explained, in the Pali discourses for a more exact definition.

I can't say whether my interpretation is any more faithful to the original intent of the Buddha, though I find it more helpful in developing awareness of one's thoughts and emotions. Instead of contracted, I would use a concept that is more functional for me, which is focused. The notion of being focused can have both a negative and a positive attribution. The negative side is that it would be rigid, narrow, biased, limited, and obsessive. The positive side of focused thinking would be in the area of concentration and logical coherence and consistency.

Instead of agitated or scattered thinking, I prefer to look at this process as conflicted thinking. Conflicted thinking is also both negative and positive. In a negative sense, which is more how you might experience this kind of thinking, conflicted thinking is related to those times when you feel doubt, confusion, perplexity, bewilderment, and uncertainty. I would relate this state to the hindrance of doubt rather than to the hindrance of restlessness and worry (as is done in the commentarial literature). But there may be some restlessness, agitation, worry, and regret in our conflicted thinking at times. On a positive note, I believe this type of conflicted thinking is absolutely necessary as a prod to question our beliefs, views, and practices.

Notice that conflicted thinking is not a direct opposite of focused thinking but a different kind of thinking. Since they are not opposites, there is no program for them to meet in the middle, no imperative to find balance or harmony. They are just different ways of thinking.

What would a focused state of mind look like? How would it differ from a state of mind that more readily shows desire, anger, or delusion? Instead of seeing a focused state of mind as essentially on equal footing with the three states of mind just mentioned perhaps it is a transitional state of mind, one that can be worked with in meditation and might actually lead somewhere. The Pali word translated here, *sankhitta,* can also mean "concise, brief" or "concentrated." It can refer to concise statements in our thinking that are more objective and reliable. It can refer to thoughts that are more focused and hold their objects. I could extend this definition to include logical thinking. The downside of being extremely focused on a topic or issue is that you may believe in the truth and accuracy of your concise observations or your logical thinking and not question them further.

A focused state of mind may actually refer to a state of mind that can come about when you get more settled and potentially more concentrated in meditation. It would therefore be a transitional state out of your ordinary worldly preoccupations and into a calmer state of mind where you can concentrate better. It may even be a state of mind that enables you to calmly explore painful areas or issues.

The Mind Grown Great

I will only briefly describe the next set of four contrasting mind states. If I were to say more about them in relation to the text of the third foundation of mindfulness, I would go into speculation and conjecture. I will simply state how I believe these mind states can be looked at in a relevant way for practicing awareness of thoughts, emotions, and states of consciousness.

The mind state of "a mind grown great" has been interpreted in a variety of ways. The most common interpretation is that it refers to a beneficial or skillful *samadhi* state and is synonymous with *samma samadhi*. Some people may take it literally as referring to an expansive or spacious state of mind, while others may take it figuratively to mean a lofty or exalted state. The word *great* in Pali does not refer to grandiosity or conceit, as there are other words for that, but it can be used to denote something as being above the ordinary. In modern parlance, we might called these mental states "higher states of consciousness." That definition is actually broad enough and sufficiently clear to suit the investigation into these states. There could be all sorts of experiences of heightened consciousness, so that what we are looking at here is a vast range of meditative states.

The Unsurpassable

The unsurpassable state of mind is a definite reference to a fully awakened, completely liberated state of mind. It is the highest, purest state of mind possible and is known only by the Buddha and arhats. If you were an arhat, you could therefore talk about it from having known it, and you should be able to recognize its absence in others. Since I do not talk about what I do not have an experience of, I would have to be silent about this mental state. But since I have had experience with states of mind that are surpassable, I can notice those states in my meditation sittings, though they come under the heading of *samadhi* states. Seeing *samadhi* states as being surpassable is part of the discerning wisdom that the Buddha recommends regarding those states. So when you experience a *samadhi* that you feel is the highest state possible, you can reflect back on it and consider whether it can be surpassed.

Tranquillity

There is some overlap between higher states of consciousness and tranquil states of mind, but the differences between these two broad categories is discernable enough to make the distinction worthwhile. If the mind grown great is identified as *samma samadhi,* then no discernment will be made here, for tranquil states of mind are definitely *samma samadhi.* The word in Pali for this mind state, *samahita,* refers to quieting and stilling the mind. The direction is not toward greatness or expansiveness or heightened consciousness but toward the stilling of your mind on an object of absorption.

Freedom

The mind state of freedom is often associated with the fully liberated mind of the Buddha or an arhat. So it is then understood to be an absolute state of liberation from which there is no turning back. The problem with that definition is that the way the Satipatthana Sutta states the practice of becoming aware of this state of mind is that one knows liberation when it is present and knows when it is absent. If it is absolute and permanent, how can it ever be absent?

So I feel at liberty to present this state of mind as indicating periods of temporary freedom from which people's minds return to states of not being free anymore. There are many experiences meditators have that make discerning this mind state meaningful, knowing that it is not full liberation we are talking about but, rather, a temporary ceasing of something that has bound us and made us suffer in its hold over us.

Expanding Awareness through Synonyms

As much as I see the value in fuller descriptions of meditative experiences, I also realize that many times only a single word or phrase will make the most immediate sense. The section of the Satipatthana Sutta on "Mindfulness of Thoughts" uses single-word descriptions exclusively. In the Buddha's time and culture, the people who heard him speak may have had a good grasp of what each word meant. Today we have many different translations for these words and are in the situation that certain translations have stuck and lasted more than others. Instead of trying to find out which translation is best, I have found that it is better for the meditators to work with the various synonyms for these terms.

When looking through a list of synonyms in a thesaurus entry, you may find a word that matches what you want to convey better than the word you started with. Getting from that initial word to a more accurate one requires further discernment of the experience being described. A common form of exploration of experiences in meditation is to question the word you have habitually used for an experience and try to find one that fits it better. Another form of exploration in Recollective Awareness meditation is to go into a fuller, longer description of an experience and come up with words and phrases that are a bit more accurate or nuanced than what you started with. In the first approach, you are breaking open the label and looking at the experience more closely to get a more precise word for it, while in the second approach, you are creating a longer narrative (a sentence or paragraph long) of the experience and then summarizing it in a single word that effectively communicates it. In both types of exploration, you end up with a new word for an experience, and that word is most likely a synonym of the word you started with or a word found in your longer description.

Here's an example of the first approach, of cracking open a label:

I was sitting with this feeling of fear and started to notice that I was dreading work tomorrow. I stayed with the feelings of dread in my chest as my mind went into a scenario of me being shamed by my boss. It has happened before, and I felt dejected and worthless afterward. That experience actually made me withdraw, lose interest in my work, and want to find another job. But I had forgotten about that memory until I started looking at the feeling of dread of going to work the next day.

If the meditator had kept labeling his experience as "fear," he might not have noticed that his thoughts were pointing to a certain kind of fear, more specifically dreading the repeat of being shamed by his boss. By looking more closely at his thoughts and emotions, he could move from a larger category (fear) to a more accurate label for his experience (dread). This may be a bit like trying to find the right word, the best synonym, for something you are writing, where you question a word you are accustomed to using and concentrate on what you want to express, to see if another word would fit better.

The second approach, of reducing a narrative down to a single word, has more the feel of rambling and then somehow coming up with a more suitable word, as in this example: *My heart was pounding and my breathing quickened. There was no way I was going to be able to sit still with what was going on in my body. My thoughts were racing with plans of how to get up and not disturb anybody in the hall when I left. As I stayed seated and tolerated the feelings and thoughts, it occurred to me that I was in a state of panic.*

In this last example the meditator notices his experience as it unfolds, and with that information, he comes to label it as "panic." You might think that if you were in a similar situation, it would be better to label this experience as "a panic attack" when you first noticed it. For then you might have a better chance of doing something about it. But that is really not the case here. This approach to meditation is not about coming to a conclusion about your experience and then taking an action on it. It is about letting it go on and getting more familiar with it. What happens then is that you learn how to tolerate the experience of panic as it manifests physically and mentally, and then, as it becomes clearer to you what is going on, the labeling of it as "panic" may just be a word your mind goes to in order to describe the experience. When we arrive at labels this way, they are the products of our tolerance and interest in our experience rather than words that are used to control our experience.

Thus synonyms can be used to explore your thoughts and emotions, whereas the words that denote a larger category of experience, such as desire, may get in the way of exploration. The only way I have found that general words such as *desire* or *anger* facilitate exploration is when one is curious about them. That is, when they are used more as a question about what you are experiencing than a statement about it: "Is this desire? If so, what kind? What is it like? How does it work? What keeps it going?" As you can see, if you take this route of exploring general categories of experience, you will get a more accurate description of an experience and better understand what the general word means in a particular context.

This brings us back to my chief problem with the Satipatthana Sutta as it is commonly interpreted and used. That problem is how people use general terms and categories to become aware of what is going on in meditation. If a key discourse of the Buddha's says to categorize your mental states in terms of greed, hatred, and delusion and seemingly indicates that you don't have to look any deeper, then meditators may feel justified staying on the surface of their experience of thoughts and emotions. They then may distance themselves from their emotional experiences by using these terms and dismissing their thoughts as all being deluded anyhow. But I hope you can see from what I have written in this chapter that the Buddha's discourses may say something different about becoming aware of thinking in meditation.

6

The Multilinear Present Moment

An interesting way to get meditators into the so-called present moment is a trick of language combined with attending to actions as they are occurring. It is a practice called noting. This practice is best applied to physical actions that have predictable segments, such as eating. Take, for example, eating a piece of buttered toast. You pick up the piece of toast and bring it to your mouth, and in the process, you note "bringing" (often when this is taught, the gerund is duplicated: "bringing, bringing"). When you bite into the toast, you note "biting," and then when you begin chewing, you note "chewing." One step follows the next inevitably. Each action is its own encapsulated event—you are chewing for only a period of time before swallowing begins.

The word *swallowing,* for example, exactly states what is going on when swallowing. The word used to note the experience is synonymous with the experience. There is no delusion here. Saying to yourself "swallowing" while actually swallowing is knowing exactly what you are doing at that point in time. You can go through the whole day noting one continuous physical action after another. Once you begin noting mental and emotional activity, however, this practice tends to fall apart, especially if you are honest with your experience and are trying to note it accurately.

The main reason for this is that the most common category for thoughts is "thinking, thinking." Everything should fit into that one. But that's the problem with this category. It's too large. Using it leads to viewing one's experience as either "thinking" or any number of physical actions that can be more accurately noted. I believe this situation regarding noting thoughts comes from the fourth foundation of mindfulness (awareness of mental phenomena), in the section referring to awareness of the six types of sense consciousness, the six sense organs, and the six objects of sense experience. Here the mind is treated as a sense organ, functioning the same way that the eyes, ears, nose, tongue, and body do. It makes contact with its objects, being all mental activity and nothing more. Just as you would hear a bird chirping and be aware of hearing, the meditator would be instructed to note each thought as "thinking." The goal in this kind of noting practice is to become aware of the sense consciousness rather than our habitual tendency to be aware of only the sense object. It is believed that if you become more aware of the sense object, such as the birdsong, you will have desire for it. While if you are primarily aware of the sense consciousness (you cannot be aware only of the sense consciousness, for it requires a sense organ and an object in order to be conscious) and are aware that you are hearing, all sounds may be considered equal and thus not judged, and you will not have any desire for or aversion to them. This shift of attention and emphasis onto mind consciousness is supposed to occur by noting all of your thoughts as "thinking, thinking." It is thus advisable not to note the content of your thoughts, as that is putting too much emphasis on what you are thinking rather than just the process of thinking. If you then master this way of noting your thinking, you will no longer have judgments regarding thoughts, and you will have no desire for certain pleasant thoughts and no aversion to unpleasant thoughts. You will just be aware of thinking as "thinking." This is first practice of being aware of thinking that I was taught when I first arrived in Sri Lanka and got instruction in a monastery.

When I look back at the phases I went through to become aware of thinking in meditation, I can see that this technique actually helped me move from meditating on the breath, body, and senses while completely ignoring thinking to noting thinking in my meditation practice in order to have it diminish and cease. There is a way that noting "thinking, thinking" when you are thinking in meditation does bring awareness to what the experience of thinking is like from the inside. It can create a similar shift that awareness of breathing does—you know it is going on throughout the day, but just stopping to recognize it once in a while orients you differently. The same can happen when noting your thinking.

I kept meditating with awareness of thinking in order to have it diminish and eventually cease, for that seemed to be, at the time, the only way not to judge it or desire it. It was becoming clear to me that if I kept seeing my thoughts as impermanent, meaning constantly arising and vanishing, then I would not become attached to them, singly or universally. The direction of my practice was to arrive at states of no thought, the so-called nonconceptual states. This is something I will return to later in the book, but for now, I would like to go into what brought me into the next phase, of allowing thinking into my meditation sittings with greater tolerance for it.

After practicing the Mahasi method as my Sri Lankan teachers taught it for six months, I began to read Mahasi Sayadaw's own writings. I was curious about what kind of meditation instructions he would give regarding becoming aware of thoughts. In his easily available book (the other books of his that I read came out of Burma and are hard to find), *Practical Insight Meditation,* there is an intriguing series of meditation instructions that he includes in "Basic Exercise 2," which is after his famous instructions on noting the rise and fall of the abdomen as a form of mindfulness of breathing. Basic exercise 2 has to do with the fact that "other mental activities may occur between the noting of each rising and falling." Here is how he instructed people to become aware of mental activities:

If you imagine something, you must know that you have done so and make a mental note *imagining*. If you simply think of something, mentally note *thinking*. If you reflect, *reflecting*. If you intend to do something, *intending*. When the mind wanders from the object of meditation which is the rising and falling of the abdomen, mentally note *wandering*. Should you imagine you are going to a certain place, mentally note *going*. When you arrive, *arriving*. When, in your thoughts, you meet a person note *meeting*. Should you speak to him or her, *speaking*. If you imaginatively argue with that person, *arguing*. If you envision and imagine a light or color, be sure to note *seeing*. A mental vision must be noted on each occurrence of its appearance until it passes away. After its disappearance, continue with the Basic Exercise 1 by knowing, by being fully aware of each movement of the rising and falling abdomen.

In these instructions, Mahasi Sayadaw is advocating a more precise noting of mental activities. Not only that, he is having students note their mental experiences using the same type of present continuous (gerund) verb forms that they would use to note physical events. Remarkably enough, he is not introducing any Buddhist terminology or theory of mind in this noting method—students are just supposed to be noting what is going on in their thoughts in the same way they would note things going on in their outer life. What I mean by this distinction is that he is not asking people to note "desiring," which would be a mental state, but, rather, has them use descriptive terms of the imagined scene: going, arriving, meeting (someone), speaking, arguing. To do this kind of precise noting of mental activities, you would need to pause and reflect on your thoughts periodically in your meditation sitting. This isn't going to happen as naturally as being aware of bodily movements. If you shift to this kind of noting of thoughts, you will find that instead of being aware of thoughts in the present moment, which the broad note of "thinking" helps people accomplish, you will be reflecting back on your thoughts and trying to find more accurate words to describe your experience. You can do this kind of noting practice only after the mental experience has occurred; when all of your thoughts are noted as "thinking," you can just use that word without any discernment of the experience. Discernment takes time.

Another consequence of this more precise noting of thoughts is that you will become more interested in your thoughts. You might find yourself asking, "What was I just thinking about?" And then you may find yourself tracing back the thoughts to where you believe they began. In this process you might notice that you were *imagining going* to a place where you were *meeting* someone whom you ended up *arguing* with (using Mahasi Sayadaw's example). Even though the Mahasi method uses the continuous "ing" ending, in the present tense, in practice, if one tried to be aware of such thoughts in the present moment, they would be interrupted and stopped by the intention to notice them. That is, if you became aware of going somewhere in your imagination, your noting of that thought would essentially put a halt to the whole imagination. One of the effects of noting is replacing one thought with another, which, in this case, happens when the noticing of the thought of going somewhere replaces the thought of meeting someone (which would have followed had the thought not been noted, in this example at least). I tried practicing this kind of precise noting of thoughts on many occasions through several meditation sittings and came up with the same result every time: noting a thought stops the thought process from progressing further. That is why noting "thinking" every time one has a thought has the apparent effect of stopping thoughts.

What I concluded from this exercise is that the only way to practice a precise noting of thoughts was to note them after the fact and trace them back. Present-moment awareness of thinking to the same degree of accuracy as noticing bodily movements was not possible. Whereas with bodily movements I knew the proper sequence beforehand and had words for each part of the sequence, with thinking I could not know the sequence beforehand and did not have adequate language for many of the thoughts and feelings I was experiencing.

Though I admire Mahasi Sayadaw for not using Buddhist terminology in his instructions on awareness of thinking, I don't think his concrete descriptive wording of thought events was adequate. By only describing a process or event that was occurring in your imagination, such as "meeting someone," so much about the experience was left out of awareness. It excluded what I and most people would be most aware of in the thinking: who I was meeting, why I was meeting this person, what I wanted from meeting this person, and so on. It also excludes the emotion or mood that is present. From my experience of listening to people report on their meditation sittings, I would say it is far more common for people to speak of feeling anxious, angry, upset, bored, and so on than for anyone to relate that she met this person and that person in her sitting. What people generally recall from their meditation sittings is what made the most impact.

As a monk, however, I did go quite a distance in training myself to note my experience in more precise descriptions, and I owe a debt of gratitude to the Mahasi method for getting me interested in looking at my thoughts in meditation from a process-oriented perspective. But when I would interview meditation students, I would generally ask for more description than a single-word note could provide. What I see as being of value in becoming aware of thoughts and emotions in meditation are descriptions that include as many parts of an experience as you can remember. So the type of description I would hear (continuing with the example from Mahasi Sayadaw) would be more in this vein: "I was imagining meeting an old friend I don't care for anymore (*meeting*). I started telling him all the things that have upset me about his behavior (*speaking*), particularly an incident that happened last May (*remembering*). I imagined him defending himself, and I was getting angry that he wasn't listening to me (*arguing*)." Though these single-word descriptors may seem to work fine as brief summaries of the thoughts, they actually tend to obscure the complex and dynamic nature of the thinking. Such labels have the tendency to get people to perceive thoughts as entities, like physical objects, that can be moved about, discarded, eliminated. The fuller descriptions, however, allow the thoughts to remain fluid, changing, and mutually dependent.

Sequences or Conditions

That *biting* into a sandwich precedes *chewing,* which in turn is followed by *swallowing,* is a step-by-step process. This can generally be the case for physical actions where the initial action must be followed by a predictable and necessary subsequent action. In most instances, biting into a sandwich leads to swallowing. It is only when the food is spit out that swallowing does not follow.

Many meditators are taught that mental processes are also simple step-by-step processes, especially in Vipassana teachings. The most common authoritative sequence comes from the Madhupindika (Honey Ball) Sutta. In a distilled form, the sequence goes like this: "The contact of sensory data gives rise to feeling, which gives rise to perceiving, thinking, and proliferating fabrications."

At first glance, this step-by-step sequence may seem to be of the same order as "biting, chewing, swallowing," but it isn't. It appears that way to us because of how we conceptualize such sequences as being composed of separate "entities," like dominoes that strike one another and then that one strikes another, and so on down the line. In various Vipassana methods, the meditator's task becomes to see these steps as separate entities and train his mind to stop at feeling and perceiving and not to enter into thinking, for that will inexorably lead to mental proliferation of fabrications.

This domino theory of how thinking runs rampant is rarely, if ever, questioned. It seems to align itself with the popular notion of triggers for traumatic experiences and the consequent search for how to respond differently to those triggers so that we don't experience the unpleasantness that follows. I think most people believe that the proper course of action here is to trace back the thoughts and emotions to where they were triggered—and when that happens, the idea seems to be not to let the mind move into the accustomed areas that it is triggered to go into, such as anxious and scary thoughts.

With this Buddhist step-by-step process, the idea becomes *not* to trigger thinking. Because if thinking is triggered, it will most likely lead to fabricating (secondary elaboration on the thinking). The idea is not to go beyond thinking but simply not to trigger it. This is to be accomplished, as the logic goes, by holding your attention on the breath or any of the five external senses. Feelings of the sense experience's being pleasant, unpleasant, or neutral are considered unavoidable, and having some vague idea (perception) of what you are sensing is part of the package, while stepping into thinking is certainly to be avoided at all costs. Why? Because if thinking is allowed, it is believed it will not stop—it will lead to deluded thoughts, unwholesome thoughts, evil thoughts, wrong thoughts, and so on.

I completely accepted this teaching in my early days as a Vipassana meditator. Most Vipassana meditators have viewed thinking in this way, as the enemy, and so have many people who have read books on meditation. One could say it is the established teaching on thinking in meditation. Debunking it is not so easy. We are halfway there just by realizing how this came to be supported by a step-by-step process of mental processes that is supposed to mirror physical processes.

First of all, isn't the whole process of a sense impression leading to thinking happening so fast that you can't stop it? You can notice it only after it has occurred. Hearing a door slam shut and thinking about who slammed it may happen so fast as to be indistinguishable. It is reasonable to assume that the physical sensation of the door slamming occurred before the thoughts about it, for how could thinking about the door slamming occur before you heard it slam? But how much sooner could it be? A fraction of a second? In that fraction of a second, could you have inserted your awareness of the sound in such a way as not to wonder who slammed the door? Would that be a reasonable thing to expect of yourself?

I would say that if the time between the sense experience and the thought is so negligible as to give an impression of their being simultaneous, then there is no possibility of stopping the thought from forming. The only way for the thought not to form is for you to be in a state of mind where you don't think thoughts about who slammed the door when you hear a door slam. But most of the time we live in states of mind where we have thoughts about what we are aware of, and those thoughts arise regardless of whether we endorse them or not.

Once thinking has arisen, there is no going back to no thought. The idea that there was a pure experience of hearing a sound and that no thought needed to form upon that experience contradicts the reality of hearing a sound and immediately thinking about it. You can't erase an experience that has already happened. But you can rewrite it according to how you conceive it to be. You can rewrite your experience of hearing the door slam along these lines: there was a moment of hearing the sound followed by a moment of thinking and then several moments of fabrication and elaboration, ending with a familiar story of how you think too much in meditation and have a hard time getting back to the present moment.

There is no pure sense experience to get back to. We can't go in reverse and change our experience. We can only go forward. And the direction forward is not to try to eliminate future thinking by attempting to stay with our sense experience in such a way as not to engender thinking. Going forward is to become aware of thinking as thinking.

This forward direction beckons us to examine the nature of linear, step-by-step progressions and see that they are an inadequate form of description for mental events. It is not the way things unfold in the mind. Our mind is much more messy and chaotic; there is greater randomness and there are more possibilities than linear descriptions can cope with. Perceptions, sensations, and emotions all intermingle with thoughts, influencing our thinking and being influenced by it. Long trains of thought are punctuated by sense impressions, such as hearing sounds, and it is not necessary to cut them short by attempts to bring your attention back to the breath. A more accurate model for this process would by necessity be in several dimensions rather than just two—discursive thinking is rarely a straight line issuing from the same source. It only appears that way when you have an identifiable trigger for the thoughts.

There are some things to consider about these sequential processes that are ascribed to the Buddha. They appear linear primarily because of the restrictions of language. When it is said that "the feeling tone of an experience arises dependent on sense contact," it sounds as though feeling follows sense contact. It can mean "the feeling tone requires sense contact"—it depends on sense contact. The emphasis is not on a sequence of events unfolding in time, one after another, but on the arising of physical and mental processes that are necessary for us to experience the world as we do. For you to experience a pleasant feeling, there has to be some kind of sense experience that it depends on, such as a sound you like, a taste you enjoy, a memory of a happy time.

The new frame I am presenting is looking at such chains of conditions as descriptions of whole structures of experience. It is not one domino hitting another but an accordion in which each distinct element is fused to the ones on either side of it. With the arising of the first one, all the others must arise—there is no separation between them. For example, the separation that we are taught exists between the feeling tone and desire, which are two adjacent links in the standard twelve-link chain of Dependent Arising, is purely conceptual.

The chain of Dependent Arising, being the standard model of causality in Buddhist teachings, originates with ignorance. Since ignorance is the first link, everything that arises with it, out of necessity, is based on ignorance. All of the physical and mental activities that rest on it are infused with this ignorance. The final elements in this chain all pertain to some kind of hurt, pain, suffering, loss, so that we can begin to get the picture that the pain in our lives is bound up with our ignorance.

A Linear Meditation Sitting

Kevin has been meditating for two years. He started off with mindfulness practice and got deeply interested in learning more about how that practice is done in the East. He is young and enthusiastic about noting each moment of his experience and having it relate directly to the truths of the Buddha's teaching as he has been taught them.

Seated cross-legged on a flat cushion, he straightens his back with an in breath. He hears the bell beginning the sitting.

"My abdomen falls with the out breath."

"Keep your attention on the rise/fall," the meditator voice commands.

"Nothing is happening. I can't feel my abdomen rise. I know I am breathing. There it is, I can feel it now." His skin feels taut and firm as it rounds its way up to the rise.

"Rising, rising," notes the meditator voice.

His skin begins to sag and moves back into a concave form.

"Falling, falling," the meditator voice says.

An itch forms on his upper lip. It is unpleasant.

"I want to scratch it," he thinks

"Keep your attention on the rise/fall," the meditator voice commands.

The skin across his abdomen rises like the dough of a baking loaf of bread; the final point is hard and crusty.

"Rising, rising," notes the meditator voice.

A memory of sitting at the sidewalk café near his house, having coffee on a sunny Sunday morning, nibbling on a croissant. The taste of the coffee, the flakiness of the croissant, and its buttery flavor all are present in his memory.

"You almost missed the falling, falling," the meditator voice says, as only the ending of the falling is felt.

"Thinking, thinking," the voice adds.

What does the note "thinking, thinking" tell us about Kevin's experience? It says very little. First of all, we don't know which experience of thinking is being referred to here. But that may not matter if the purpose of the note is to bring awareness to all of those recent instances where your attention strayed from the primary object of meditation, being awareness of breathing at the abdomen. If we break down some of the elements that are being subsumed under thinking, we find metaphors (skin rising like a loaf of bread), memories (Sunday morning at the neighborhood café), and that meditator voice ("You almost missed the falling, falling") to name some of the more obvious thoughts.

The metaphor of baking bread was a thought that arose from being aware of the sensation of his abdomen rising. It faithfully followed the sequence of sense contact, feeling, perceiving, thinking, and proliferation of fabrication. He could have traced back the sequence of experiences and put it into that conceptual model. The memory of the Sunday morning coffee and croissant could also be seen as faithfully following the sequence, though you have to squeeze the memory into the sequence, since, as a memory, it is not actually a fabrication or an elaboration. It is a memory that followed as a train of associations stemming from the metaphor. It seems so orderly, as these experiences often do when you have been conditioned to see them as linear sequences. Putting this kind of meditation sitting into another form is perhaps really not possible—the view of linear development, which is further augmented by a linear practice of following the breath, conditions not only how Kevin conceives his experience but also how it unfolds.

What will upset this orderliness is greater awareness of your experience. Your experience will appear less orderly when you stop practicing mindfulness. That is a given. It does not mean you will revert back to what you were like before you undertook mindfulness practice. And for those who have never practiced mindfulness, you will become aware of other ways you have managed, controlled, organized, and otherwise ordered your inner experience. Those ways may have come from doing certain therapies or religious practices, thinking things through, or just growing up in a society that teaches people to get their inner worlds to function in an orderly manner.

This noting practice, along with other mindfulness practices, does succeed in bringing people more in touch with their breath, bodily sensations and movements, and sense experiences. Those practices help create a strong awareness of those parts of our experience and can be more effective at doing this than Recollective Awareness meditation. Whenever I am asked to lead a retreat or activity where mindfulness practices would seem most appropriate, I have to get creative and stretch the practice of Recollective Awareness to fit within that context. That is what I did in 2011 when I was invited to teach meditation on a "yatra."

The Australian Yatra

Traditionally, in India and Nepal, a yatra is a pilgrimage to a holy place. The holy place on this yatra was Mount Gulaga, a mountain sacred to the Aborigines, located on the eastern coast of Australia 370 kilometers south of Sydney. In Australia and other Western countries, a yatra is a group backpacking (bushwalking) trip that involves periods of yoga, meditation, and, in this case, swimming in the ocean. The leaders were Victor von der Hyde and Ronnie Hickel, and it was organized by Jane Dwyer and her partner, Peter Byrne. I have known Victor for some years, and he had invited me to teach on this particular yatra, though I could be on it for only four days.

Initially, I was faced with a very interesting problem regarding teaching awareness on this yatra. People would be expecting talks and instructions on being in the present moment. At least, I would if I were they. If I were taking off work for two weeks of hiking through beautiful country and swimming in warm, clear, and clean ocean water, I might want all of my senses soaking it up and not have to be in my head.

Would the people on this yatra react negatively to looking at their thoughts and feelings? Would they find it *not* what they signed up for? The reason I even asked myself these questions was that I have felt myself to be like a small island in a large ocean of "being in the now." What people seem to want when it comes to being in nature is a way to become completely absorbed in nature.

As it turned out, this group was fine with not getting mindfulness instructions. They didn't need to be told to be aware of each moment of their feet moving, especially when walking across boulders and rocks along the coast—you had to be aware of where you were placing your feet, as it was easy to slip or fall if you weren't careful. When we came to beautiful vistas—the views from the pastureland on hills overlooking the ocean were just stunning—it was hard not to be absorbed in the scenery. When swimming in the surf or in a still lagoon, the feel of the water and air was so special, everyone's senses were alive in the experience. People's awareness of what they were experiencing was happening of its own, and between those periods, as people walked in silence, it was okay for them to think about things that had nothing to do with being on the yatra. Only a couple people expressed the wish that they could have been more present, more available to the beauty around them, but they too saw the benefit in being able to be gentle and allowing of their thoughts and feelings as they walked, ate, pitched their tents, and talked to each other as the day faded into dusk.

The first long talk I gave was titled the "Shorter *Sutta* on Emptiness." I wrote it down beforehand, which is the only reason I can now reproduce it faithfully for you.

"Here on this yatra, your life is empty of e-mail, phone conversations, work to be done, the various activities of your home life. With that emptiness, other things arise, such as remembering your daily jobs, where you left your bowl and eating utensils, when to be silent and when you can talk again; being aware of where you step; and so on. Our lives have this quality of being empty of some things for a while, replaced by other things. So it is with our inner world in meditation—we may have periods of being empty of certain mundane and ordinary thoughts but find ourselves aware of our bodily sensations, sounds, inner images, or inner quiet. Our experience in meditation has this dynamic quality of change, where we become empty of something that is then replaced by something else.

"During the day you are no doubt shifting from one mental state to another, with no one state remaining constant—fears, sadness, irritation, and excitement last for a bit of time, and then you move on. Meditation can heighten this process of one thing arising and passing away, and another thing arising, where it may move faster and be easier to see and navigate. This leads to a truth of the Buddha's teaching: there is no single state of mind we live in all the time. That is, there is no stable, enduring self. Such statements as "I am an anxious person" or "I am a depressed person" are labels given to one part of our experience, but there is no way for us to be always anxious or always depressed.

"Those of you who shared the other night that your challenge in life is your own mind speak for all of us."

This ending note keeps haunting me each time I read it: "Your challenge in life is your own mind." It reminds of me a verse in the Rig Veda that reads, "I do not clearly know what I am like here; bewildered and bound by mind, I wander." To me, this addresses the question of where we put our attention for the most benefit. Do we put it on the present moment? Or do we put it on knowing what I am like here? Courageously looking at the challenges your mind presents, the bewildering periods, the periods of being bound (to anxiety, depression, delusion, you name it)—that is a legitimate practice of self-knowledge.

A couple of days later I gave another talk, this one called "The *Sutta* to Vacchagotta on (the Symbolic Meaning of) Fire."

The wanderer Vacchagotta visits the Buddha in Savatthi and asks him, "How is it, Master Gotama, do you hold the view, 'the universe is eternal; only this is true, anything otherwise is deluded?'"

The Buddha replies that he does not hold the view that the universe is eternal. Vacchagotta then assumes the Buddha holds the opposite view, that the universe in not eternal. And the Buddha replies that he does not hold that view either. This goes on for another eight views, until Vacchagotta then catches on and asks the Buddha, "Seeing what drawback, then, is Master Gotama not taking up any of these views?"

The Buddha replies rather definitively. He says that the taking up of such views is a thicket of views, a fetter of views. It is accompanied by suffering, distress, despair, and fever and does not lead to calm, full awakening, liberation of mind.

Vacchagotta asks, "Does Gotama have any view at all?"

The Buddha replies, "A view is something the Buddha has done away with. What a buddha sees is this: such is form, such is its origin, such is its cessation (and the same with consciousness, feeling, perception, and habit formations). With the ending, fading out, cessation, renunciation, and relinquishment of all construing, all mental fabrication, all self-production, possessiveness, and comparing with others—it is through lack of sustenance given to these that one is released."

Vacchagotta asks, "The monk whose mind is thus released, where does he reappear?"

The Buddha says, "Reappear doesn't apply to him."

Vacchagotta admits, "I am confused. The clarity coming to me from a previous conversation is now obscured."

The Buddha says, "Of course you are confused. Deep is this Dhamma, hard to see, hard to realize, tranquil, refined, beyond reasoning, subtle, to be experienced by the wise."

The Buddha continues, "If a fire is burning in front of you, would you know that this fire is burning in front of you?"

"Yes."

"Dependent on what is it burning?"

Vacchagotta replies, "Dependent on grass and twigs as its fuel."

"If it were to go out, would you know that it went out?"

"Yes."

Buddha then says, "Suppose someone asked you in which direction has it gone? Did it go to the east, west, north, or south?"

"That doesn't apply," Vacchagotta says. "From having consumed that sustenance and not being offered any other, it is simply known as 'extinguished.'"

In this dialogue, the Buddha is using fire and the fuel that it relies on as a metaphor to describe where your attention is best placed: on the fire burning in front of you. You could say that is the same as being in the present moment, but that really isn't the case. Paying attention to this mental state before you and how it is fed requires looking into the past as well as the future. That is something I will go into in the next chapter.

Multilinear Point of View

I would prefer not to conceptualize how I see consciousness working in meditation, but it seems unavoidable. In earlier chapters I have stated that I don't see mental events as progressing only in a linear fashion. To be more precise, I don't believe our experience flows in a single line, but, rather, it moves along multiple lines, and occasionally those lines intersect and affect each other.

In agreement with Buddhist notions of linear causality, I see that when a process is set in motion, it moves in a particular direction. In terms of mental processes, when you have an idea to do something, that idea moves in a particular direction, but the steps it goes through in that direction are not strictly determined. For example, if you have an idea you want to write down, but not the precise wording of it, you will probably begin writing and find that certain words and phrases come to mind that express that idea for you. But that is not the only way to write down that idea—you could have found other words and phrases and a whole different writing style that might have gotten the same idea across. The direction—by which I mean the momentum and trajectory of the thought process—can pass through different ideas and emotions on its way to express the one idea you have in mind. That is to say, I do not believe there is a single sequence of mental events that one can apply to each and every thought process. There is merely a thought process that is set in motion and goes in a particular direction. This thought process has no beginning to it and no end to it.

My last statement may sound a bit metaphysical, but it is actually a very practical and useful observation on thought processes. I believe we do not know the origin of most of our habitual trains of thought for they are a combination of thought processes, and to disentangle them is not really possible. Can you remember the first time you rehearsed a conversation, planned your day, or mulled over a difficult problem? Somehow you just started doing these things, and they have been going on ever since. These are thought processes that get set in motion, and you enter into them as though they had been going along all the time. What if, in some way, each kind of thought process, even down to the particular subject and feeling tone it has, were continuing along its own line, following its own direction? We may think that the thought process of mulling something over has an end when we have a solution, but then why does it come back again and again? By its not having an end, I am referring to the recurring nature of the thought process. Even if we reach a conclusion regarding the idea or the problem we are trying to solve, that thought process is bound to recur.

Getting back to the concept of multilinear thought processes, I believe that if we see our mind as operating on many linear tracks, we may be able to see more clearly how we jump from one track to another, rather than having the illusion of one track ending and another beginning. It is this view that a thought ends before another arises (or a sensation ends before a thought arises) that I believe goes against what the Buddha saw as the law of Dependent Arising: "when this arises, that also arises . . . ; when this ceases, that also ceases." As a simple example, when you think about work, a certain train of thought arises about what you must get done, and when you don't think about work, the train of thought about what you must get done at work also doesn't arise. But that doesn't mean it ceases altogether; it just doesn't arise until the conditions are such for it to arise again. For such thoughts to truly cease, you may have to retire from work and not go back.

This simple model of multilinearity that I am presenting does get more complicated when one linear thought process interacts with another line of thought. When you concentrate on something, whether it is an idea, a visual image, your breath, or even a problem, you are trying to keep one line of thought (or focused attention) from being distracted by other lines of thought. When you can't concentrate on the breath or anything specific, sometimes your thoughts will go all over the place, following one train of thought or another, which is much like what happens when people practice Recollective Awareness meditation. But since you are meditating, you are most likely looking for something to concentrate on, and so you find a train of thought that holds your interest. This train of thought will most likely be accompanied by bodily sensations, emotions, or a mood. It may have views and values. Those elements may seem to solidify around the train of thought and make it seem more three-dimensional—there isn't only thinking but a sense of yourself having a much fuller experience. But you can't hold that experience for long without another train of thought presenting itself that seems to replace the previous train of thought or interact with it. This metaprocess occurs very often in meditation.

A Multilinear Meditation Sitting

Julian has been meditating for about six months. He is a neat and organized middle-aged man who lives alone and is a lawyer for an environmental law firm. He came to meditation because he couldn't get out of his head and believed his life was passing him by. He wants to have a long-term relationship with a woman but is too shy to go out and meet people. He prefers to spend his free time reading or watching movies and usually goes hiking alone on the weekends. He meditates for forty minutes a day, usually in the morning, and then twice a week in the evening when he attends the local sitting group.

Inside Julian's meditation sitting:

"A fan is humming loudly, or is that the refrigerator? I can't seem to get comfortable with my legs crossed on the floor. I wish I had sat in a chair. But they were all taken. That is what I get for arriving a couple of minutes late. The early bird catches the worm. What a strange notion. But I do have to be first in everything. I should be the best meditator here, but I'm probably not even close."

He brings his attention to his sitting posture, feels his body from the inside for a few seconds, and then takes two deep breaths.

"I don't meditate enough—I don't go on enough retreats. I haven't been on any retreat longer than a weekend. I must sign up for a ten-day retreat."

He feels some pressure in his chest and focuses on it for a moment.

"I saw one I liked in the catalog from that big retreat center up north. It was a singles' retreat."

He sees a picture of a young woman with long, curly blond

hair and a sweet oval face with a warm bright smile—her white teeth shine brighter and brighter for some seconds before vanishing altogether, leaving behind tingling sensations in his chest.

"Yes, I must do that retreat. I will meet her, or someone like her. But how is that done with ten days of silence? I don't know. Maybe it is just a gimmick to get lonely people to attend a longer retreat. My cynical side stepping in to ruin things, smash my dreams. If I don't go on a retreat during my vacation, then where will I go?"

He settles in to feeling the weight of his right hand resting on his left in his lap as a calmness rises to fill his whole body.

"I can just see myself sitting by a pool in a hotel in someplace like Waikiki, all alone, waiting for someone to come up to me."

He feels a sensation of pressure returning to his chest, but this time it increases and feels as if it were stabbing him.

"This feeling of being unlovable is too painful for me."

He feels the stabbing sensation move down his chest to his waist, where it burns even hotter.

"I can't bear it, but I must sit through it."

He feels some tears well up.

"It will never work out. I will never meet her. I will forever be alone."

He then experiences a moment of stepping out of these thoughts and glancing back at them.

"Do I really believe that about myself?"

There is nothing that he is doing that reenforces the notion that all of his experience is going in a straight line—he is not bringing his attention back to his breath or doing any prescribed meditation instruction. I can list his thoughts in linear order for the sake of convenience, but it will be shown that one thought is not inexorably following another. Instead, they form different multilinear tracks.

1. He has to be first in everything and feels he should be the best meditator there.
2. He doesn't meditate enough and hasn't been on enough retreats.

3. He wants to go on a ten-day retreat.
4. He wants to meet a single woman on a retreat.
5. An image of a woman he would like to meet appears in his mind.
6. Maybe the singles' retreat idea is a gimmick. His cynical side steps in.
7. He thinks about where to go on his vacation: either on a retreat or to a Waikiki resort.
8. He pictures himself on vacation all alone.
9. He feels unlovable and can't bear it.
10. He starts to feel that he will always be alone and never meet the woman in the image that arose.
11. He experiences a moment of stepping out of his thoughts.
12. He questions whether he believes the whole narrative he has been spinning.

As I read through the fictional sitting to create this list, I noticed that some of these thoughts could be bound up together, even though Julian was jumping from one track to another and another or back again throughout the whole sitting. For example, numbers 4, 5, 8, 9, and 10 seem to cluster around a longing to meet a woman who could be his life partner. The thought process starts with the hope that he will meet somebody, which turns into a desire to meet a particular woman whose image came to him, and then in its trajectory, the thought process hooks up with an emotional process of feeling lonely, unlovable, and perhaps a bit depressed. In between there were 6 and 7, where he was cynical and perhaps a bit superior in comparing himself with others, which can link up with the thoughts of having to be first in everything that he was having at the beginning of the sitting. So here are two probable linear tracks, each with its own separate development, that are first pursued, then forgotten, and then returned to at another place in their trajectory. It is as if the thoughts of being superior were going to lead to thoughts of being cynical and nothing was going to get in the way of that—just as his thoughts about meeting a woman were bound to lead him to feeling lonely and unlovable, because that is where such trains of thought usually lead him.

So hopefully you have some idea of how at least two different tracks of thinking can go off and on in a meditation sitting. What makes this even more complex is how the trains of thought were interacting with each other, with emotions and sensations, and with how the meditator was relating to them. Starting with the first two tracks of thinking, the thoughts of self-inflation and deflation at the beginning of the sitting affected his thoughts about meeting a woman. But in this case, she was special and he was hopeless. There was a bleeding through of his initial sense of superiority and inferiority into much of his thinking. It was lurking within the thoughts, behind the scenes until it came onstage. If he had picked this up earlier in the sitting, the sitting might have progressed without this being such an influential feature.

I didn't mention his emotions and sensations in the sitting in the list of thoughts, but I could have. If I add those in, we first find him feeling a pressure in his chest as he thinks about signing up for a ten-day retreat. Could he be anxious about getting into the retreat? If so, then this emotion belongs to another track, that of not getting something he wants and the fear of that. So if we track this pressure in his chest, it seems to go away for some time in the sitting, returning when he imagines himself on vacation all alone, where it becomes a stabbing sensation that spreads down his torso when he starts believing that he is unlovable. The momentum in the feeling of being anxious about not getting something he wants (a room at the singles' retreat) grows and builds into a feeling of being unlovable, which ties in with the track of thinking that he is unlovable and will always be alone and may really be indistinguishable from it. If he stayed with the emotion/sensation and observed how it interacted with his thoughts, he might have seen how he was elaborating on a feeling of not getting something he wanted and felt he deserved, linking that up with a familiar self-story of being unlovable.

Since I am not advocating changing your experience in meditation by doing a technique or employing a strategy, the way your meditation practice moves in a healthy and wise direction is through how you relate to the different trains of thoughts and emotions. As you can see in Julian's meditation sitting, he is not resisting any aspect of his experience. He lets his thoughts go on without bringing them back to his breath and holds his attention on his body only when there is a sensation that has called his attention. He is accustomed to being receptive and is trusting that it will lead somewhere. And it does. At the very end of the sitting, the awareness, discernment, and wisdom that he has been slowly cultivating in his meditation practice help him step out of these thoughts and glance back at them: "Do I really believe that about myself?"

7

Going Into the Future and the Past

The whole notion of going into the future has always bothered me. How do thoughts go into the future? Do they somehow leave the moment of their occurrence and travel through time? It seems to be a notion that any thought about the future must somehow be directing one's attention to the future and taking one away from the present. Then people should say that in the present moment they are thinking about the future. The thought that goes into the future lives in the present. It too could become something one is aware of in the present, if only being aware of thoughts in the present were possible. Since, like most thoughts, a thought about the future is known in recollection (either immediate or after some time has passed), the future-oriented thought is more often known as something that has already affected one's present experience.

In practice, future-oriented thinking may be more accurately described as planting memories of intentions to have certain things happen in the future. If I am thinking about something I need to do later, such as prepare dinner, then my thinking about dinner turns into a plan for dinner, one that I can either follow, modify, or reject. What I am producing is in fact a memory of what I intend to prepare for dinner or a reminder that I need to do certain things in order to make dinner. You can look at most of your going-into-the-future thoughts as planting intentions, reminders, solutions, and decisions, which you most likely intend to reference at some later date. It is the imagining of that later date, and what should occur on that date, that gives the illusion that you are going into the future.

I am sure many of you believe that you know what someone will say or how the person will react to something you plan to say or do, so you don't say and do certain things because of that fated outcome. You may even go over such imagined conversations in meditation, one scenario after another. You move from angry, upset, and demanding toward kind, open, and fair-minded and then get thrown back again into some kind of agitation, from which you either emerge with what you will say or do or go through another round. While all of this is going on, you are not in the future by any means—you are with thoughts and emotions that are arising and shifting in the present.

Planning

In practicing Recollective Awareness meditation, you may find yourself at times conflicted about whether to continue planning during a meditation sitting or redirect your attention away from the planning. This struggle arises partly because planning during meditation has not been allowed in the past. You may still believe it is not okay to plan while you meditate. If you don't really believe that it is okay to make plans while meditating, then you will constantly encounter this struggle when your mind begins to make plans. The resistance to planning may also be reinforced by the belief that true meditation is being in the present moment. Are you ready and willing to question the belief that planning *does not* belong in meditation?

Let's say you have come around to the belief that planning is okay in meditation, at least during some sittings and with certain topics, which is a fairly realistic and honest place to get to. Then you might find that you have less added conflict and struggle when it is okay to do some kinds of planning, while there is still conflict about allowing other kinds of planning. I am not trying to get you to have a blanket acceptance of planning in meditation but, rather, an awareness of what types of planning you can tolerate and what types you can't.

One good thing about noticing that you are planning in meditation is that you can identify something distinctive in your thinking that makes it planning and not, say, generic thinking. But when someone is taught to note all future-oriented thoughts as "planning, planning," that label loses its ability to make more precise discernments regarding your thinking and thus becomes a way to categorize the experience quickly. Once one cracks open the label of "planning" and looks within it, there are potentially many complex mental processes that can be seen and explored. Let's break open this label like an orange, with ten sections in it, and look more closely at ten types of experiences that otherwise would be labeled as "planning."

1. Rehearsing a conversation (internal monologues and dialogues)
2. List making (to-do lists mostly)
3. Working on a project (building, cleaning, redecorating, designing, composing, writing, and so forth)
4. Organizing (event planning, contemplating a purchase, planning a vacation)
5. Hoping or wishing something will happen (including pleasant daydreams)
6. Sexual fantasy (as contrasted with a sexual memory)
7. Violent fantasy (as contrasted with a violent memory)
8. Dread and apprehension (worrisome or paranoid thoughts)
9. Ambitious thoughts (thoughts of doing great things and becoming someone)
10. Hopeless thoughts (thoughts of failure, withdrawing, suicide)

By discerning different kinds of planning, instead of seeing all types of planning as the same, you may see what kinds are okay with you and why that is so, what kinds are less acceptable or are questionable, and those that are completely unacceptable. Suppose you are mentally working on a project while meditating and find those thoughts acceptable. Later on in the meditation sitting you notice yourself rehearsing a conversation with someone at work and deem that thought as less acceptable. Then there may be a value judgment on the thinking that makes working on a project seem fine and unproblematic, while rehearsing what you intend to say to someone seems to be of questionable value. You can be receptive to the work project, maybe because it can be creative and productive, but not to the internal dialogue. Why is that? Is it because the internal dialogue goes on and on? That it brings up uncomfortable feelings? That it is boring? That you believe it is unnecessary? You would not have been able to ask such questions if you had not discerned the difference between these two types of planning.

Now let's take a closer look at some of the questionable types of planning. Suppose making to-do lists is okay when it is efficient and productive but not okay when it gets obsessive. So, in this situation, you might feel as though you should either stop making lists, because nine times out of ten it becomes obsessive, or allow it to go on, because it may actually be productive on occasion. This is how list making may appear to you outside meditation, when it is something you have to do every so often in order to get things done. When it comes to meditation, list making may seem to be such a mundane, worldly, and trivial activity, not worthy of being included in your meditation practice, that it could solely be considered unacceptable on account of its lowly nature. But if it were productive and passed quickly, then maybe it would be okay. If it becomes obsessive, where all you do is improve a single list or make one list after another for most of the meditation period, then it is certainly taking advantage of your generosity. You just don't know for sure—it's that tricky. Do you allow it, do you stop it, do you welcome it in while giving it a time to leave; what do you do? My suggestion is to do nothing about it. Let it form into an obsession; if it wants to take up your whole meditation sitting, then that is what your mind needs to do.

With obsessive thinking in meditation, you can't negotiate a deal with it, and you can't really give it the boot. Sitting with rushing thoughts that don't stop is not a very pleasant experience, most particularly when doing a meditation practice where they are supposed to stop. If you do a meditation practice where they are not supposed to stop but are allowed to go on indefinitely, then the experience is not so unpleasant and could even become tolerable.

After sitting through such a storm of thinking, when you reflect back on it, you may recall one or two things that were productive about the list making, event organizing, or vacation planning, but that is not what will be meaningful. The hidden gem in such experiences is seeing how all of this thinking about the future actually does create bits and pieces of the future if those thoughts turn into intentions to do things in the future. Even if you forget you had the intention to do something on a list you made in a meditation sitting, you might find yourself unconsciously acting on that intention when the time comes. That process is going on throughout the day, largely unnoticed and unexamined, so looking at it when reflecting back on your meditation sittings may bring in more awareness and discernment regarding such subtle intentions.

You may then wonder why I would suggest allowing the planning to go on if it is going to create intentions that you act on unawares in the future. Wouldn't it make more sense not to have the plans in the first place? For without the planning going on in your head, there would be no intentions for those future actions to take place. By stopping the planning, you would also stop the actions. So the argument goes.

If you have never pursued this argument further, it is actually here that the counterargument gets quite interesting. What happens when there are no *new* intentions regarding a future action? We may just go on automatic, follow our habits without question. Could the planning that is occurring in meditation actually be producing new intentions, some of which are distinct improvements that could then arise instead of the preexisting habits? For us to trust this process, we would have to see for ourselves how our mind in meditation can produce new beneficial intentions on its own. Usually this is done by trying to program the new better intentions through some kind of repetition of words or aspirations or by modifying thoughts and behaviors, but I am not suggesting that you do any of that.

By way of example, I would like to explore some thinking of the mundane variety, most specifically, thoughts about making a purchase. At first those plans may be judged as petty, selfish, materialistic, not the stuff that should occupy your mind in meditation. They are clearly present-moment desires that form into thoughts about what you will do in the future. Unless you are an impulsive shopper (in a meditation sitting it is much harder to be impulsive than when in a store or shopping online), you are making deliberations, weighing your needs and wants with your bank account or credit card debt, assessing whether the object of desire is really the right one and whether you are contemplating buying from the right store, trying to save yourself from buyer's remorse. This is much more complex than a simple label of "planning" would have us believe. And to top it off, while you are going through these deliberations in your meditation sitting, you wonder if you are thinking about this purchase to take your attention off something more pressing or more meaningful or whether it is some way that you tend to sooth yourself, indulge yourself. By now you may be thinking that nothing good is going to come out of all of this "planning, planning," and then you spot your impatience at work. It is a new element in the mix. It comes up to push you to make a decision, one that you will hold to, so that you can then move on. You want to get this over with. You begin to wonder if that is how you usually decide to make a purchase and whether many of your purchases are satisfying your impatience (or restlessness) rather than your needs and desires? And here, for a moment, a habitual way of being is noticed and questioned. If you did not see this in your meditation sitting by allowing the planning to go on, then you might have continued to believe that all of your purchases are made on account of desire for the object. Now you see that many of them are made on account of a desire to end the deliberations, which manifests physically and mentally as impatience and restlessness.

In this process, a new intention has not been created yet. Just be patient. Instead of replacing one intention with another, as is commonly taught, we are questioning an existing intention (habit formation) that is not working all that well for us. Restless and impatient buying can get us into trouble. But now if we know that about ourselves, we can at least be aware of a pervasive underlying mood of impatience and/or restlessness when we are contemplating a purchase, a mood that is asking to be satisfied by carrying through with it. We now know there is something off-kilter about this situation. We need to let it arise in meditation so we can look at it, around it, underneath it, at what is alongside it and what is supporting it. In all of this looking at it, it can be drained of its power, of its credibility, and of its urgency. It is satisfied without acting on it, for what is gratification of desire but a feeling of satisfaction from having the desire fulfilled? Now there can be satisfaction from the desire's *not* being fulfilled, which, in the past, has usually been a source of displeasure, frustration, disappointment, and so on.

Planning That Is Deemed Unacceptable

From my earlier list, I would hazard that sexual and violent fantasies, dread and apprehension, and hopeless thoughts are deemed unacceptable by most meditators. The reason I can make this broad generalization is that they are usually left out of people's journals and interviews. It is very rare for a meditation student to volunteer that he or she has been meditating with such thoughts. And if no one talks about it, then it becomes an area that everyone keeps silent about, and you then find that none of the experts on meditation address it except to say that you should not feed such thoughts and should always bring your attention to a more wholesome, acceptable theme, which creates an atmosphere of shame and secrecy around such thoughts.

Usually, if someone has been in psychotherapy, there is a willingness to talk about dread and apprehension as well as depression and hopelessness. But if the symptoms are getting worse while meditating and there is no end in sight, the person feeling fear and apprehension may not want to let the teacher know. For letting the teacher know may bring up feelings of shame and failure. This is why it may be useful to write about this in a book on meditation, so some people can get help from the meditation practice without needing to reveal the depths of their anguish, shame, and suffering to the teacher. I do advise, however, that anyone experiencing a progressive worsening of psychological pain while meditating, or a steady and constant high level of emotional pain, seek professional help.

ANXIETY AND DEPRESSION

I don't know anyone who hasn't experienced some form of anxiety or depression in his or her life. Meditation teachings from the East are for the mentally healthy and were not created to combat mental illness, though some practitioners of old had their share of being attacked or possessed by hostile influences. I have heard superstitious beliefs that opening your mind up in meditation, as I teach it, will also open people up to negative influences. When one is going through a period of depression or anxiety, meditation practices can either help manage it or feed it and make it worse.

Mindfulness meditation and Recollective Awareness meditation are focused more on how you are with your depressed mood and/or anxiety than what you should do about it. These meditation practices are done mostly without an overt agenda, though mindfulness is a more directed meditation practice than Recollective Awareness, so there are times when someone could be directed to be mindful of a certain area of experience, such as a panic attack, with the background idea that such attention will help change it for the better. Recollective Awareness, being undirected, may still be used to become aware of a specific experience, such as a panic attack, but only because that is what one is experiencing at the time. The emphasis would be on how you are relating to the panic, namely, whether you are able to be gentle with it or are trying to subdue it. The same might be true with mindfulness practices. With Recollective Awareness you are allowing the panic attack to unfold and progress as it would naturally—learning how to tolerate the sensations, thoughts, and emotions as your panic fluctuates between bearable and intense—and then at some point you may pick up some of the more hidden features of your panic experience and be able to explore them inside the meditation sitting or afterward when you reflect back on your sitting. This way of allowing anxious and/or depressed moods and thoughts into your meditation sitting may be too difficult at times, as the depression or anxiety may feel overwhelming, so at those times you may need to switch to a practice of gently bringing your attention away from your thoughts and emotions and back to your body or breath. Making that choice is not a failure. The idea here would not be to keep your attention on your breath or your body but to let your mind go back into the thoughts and emotions after you have gained some relief from having been focused on the breath or the body for a little while. You can think of being with your breath or bodily awareness at these times as being on a perch, or just taking a rest stop, before moving on again.

Recollective Awareness meditation should not be done in a rigid, inflexible manner, especially when it comes to sitting with powerfully negative thoughts and moods. To do so would be the psychological equivalent of sitting in full lotus for an hour-long meditation sitting, determined not to move, seeing freedom from suffering as going through all the pain until it dissolves. Prolonged intense mental or emotional pain will wear you down, and you may find that you are becoming hard and cold around it, not compassionate and equanimous. So, instead, be loose with the practice of being open to everything for however long it needs to run its course. That may mean halting a long train of angry, judgmental, or depressing thoughts and shifting your attention to something more neutral and calming, such as your bodily contact with the cushion, chair, or mat.

People who have suffered from prolonged depression or anxiety, unlike those who have only sporadic experiences with these moods, may find themselves anxious or depressed during several meditation sittings. They may have tried a variety of strategies to help them be with, deal with, or work with their persistent unfriendly moods but with little success outside of momentary relief. Many of these individuals are taking medication for their condition or have done so in the past or are considering it for the future. Meditating while under the care of a physician and/or psychotherapist may be the best option for such individuals, as meditation in combination with psychotherapy will most likely be more effective.

Someone's journey through depression with this meditation practice is unique to that person. The recurring sittings of depression are not a hindrance—the depressed mood is what the meditator learns to tolerate, explore, and not take up on occasion. It is not singled out but, rather, seen within the context of all the other experiences that are included in the person's practice, such as the periods of dullness, agitation, boredom, worry, and varying degrees of calm. Depression is not being targeted for removal; it is allowed to be as heavy and intractable as it feels. It just isn't the only thing one feels, contrary to how the depressed person often sees it.

Sexual and Violent Fantasies

First of all, sexual fantasies are very common during meditation, and there is nothing wrong about having them. Many people have the notion that their meditation sittings have to be pure and undefiled, like a lotus rising out of a muddy pond—all of that dirt not touching its pristine form. They may even believe that one dirty thought can pollute the whole meditation period, so it has to be expunged immediately. And since each of us has our own inner censor with its own idiosyncratic rating system, even the most open-minded fall victim to shutting down all sexual fantasies. I guess if you see your meditation period as a temple, thinking about having sex in it would feel sacrilegious.

With sexual fantasies in meditation, there are a series of lines that you might step back from and only rarely, if ever, cross, and being aware of those lines for yourself is most useful. The first line is reached when you start getting sexually aroused. Do you continue to allow the fantasies to go on and yourself to get more aroused? Or do you draw the line there? If you do draw the line at arousal, then you find yourself sitting with the discomfort of being aroused and deciding not to follow through with it. You might find that certain emotions arise with sexual fantasies, such as shame, irritation, rage, or sadness, to name a few. Your thoughts may also move away from fantasy and more toward what you are feeling and thinking about your decision not to pursue the fantasy. There may be some residual sensations from having been slightly aroused that also change now that you are no longer pursuing the fantasy. In sitting with this, you may find out some things about yourself that would never occur to you by keeping the arousal going.

This kind of meditation sitting may have the flavor of sexual tantra (without a physical partner), where you are keeping yourself from climaxing. You may find recurring images and scenes mixed in with fluctuations in arousal, and I suggest you do not intentionally feed yourself sexual images but let them arise more on their own. During this kind of sitting, it is important not to masturbate or do any type of physical arousal. It is all mental, done while in a meditation posture, with no moving of the body.

Letting the fantasy play out but without physical involvement is as far as anyone should go with sexual fantasies in meditation. And you certainly don't need to go this far in order to learn more about your sexual thoughts and fantasies. By letting your sexual fantasies play out in meditation, while maintaining a still and solid meditation posture throughout, you may begin to develop awareness of that state of mind, so that you can be more awake and aware of it when it occurs at other times.

Violent fantasies are another case altogether. Fantasies of rape, torture, murder, and so on really should not be allowed to go on for too long. Short-lived violent images are fairly commonplace in some people's meditation sittings. As long as they do not lead to full-blown fantasies and intentions, they can be tolerated in meditation. If they persist and produce any violent intentions or acting out, then it would be advisable to work with such thoughts within a professional setting with a skilled psychiatrist or psychotherapist.

There was an instance when a twenty-year-old meditator came to me with his concern about having violent fantasies in meditation. In the course of the interview, it appeared that his habit of playing computer action games, which tended to be a type of participation in violent acts, was playing out in his sittings rather than actual violent thoughts addressed to living and breathing people in his life. This, of course, is a case where what you spend your time doing outside of meditation will come into your meditation sittings. If you read, watch, or engage in some kind of sexual or violent activity, expect it to surface at times when you meditate. That is the perfect time to look at how that activity influences your thoughts.

Ambition, Grandiosity, Self-Becoming

It is hard to say no to a pleasant daydream in meditation, though many serious meditators may feel as guilty about imagining being famous, wealthy, or successful as they would about having a sexual fantasy. To imagine a future self that has material happiness is antithetical to Buddhist practice, which advocates a life of peace and happiness through nonattachment to material, worldly things. So a period of fantasizing about having fame and wealth, or even just more recognition, may be stopped because that is not why you are meditating. In fact, you may believe that you have to renounce those desires in order to progress in meditation, just like monks and nuns supposedly have. You may believe you should be satisfied with a simple life of few pleasures. That could even be one of the reasons you have stuck with meditation in the first place—it really does bring moments of peace and happiness that are not dependent on the outside world.

This is an area of great ambiguity for meditators. Do you use meditation to renounce the world? Or do you use meditation to help develop your life in the world? Where these two directions meet is in the area of learning what you may need to renounce in the world in order to help you develop your life in the world. To find that out, you will need to let your ambitions, hopes, dreams, and needs for the future come into your meditation sittings. Getting to know your thoughts on future self-becoming will help you understand what it is you really and truly want your life to become. Those thoughts may even be practical plans on how to achieve your goals. Though they might also be flights of fancy and highly improbable. It may be sufficient for some of the fantasies to be lived out only in your imagination instead of acting on them in the world. Some of your thoughts may show you what is missing or lacking in your life right now. Going into the future in this way will inevitably engender reflection on your life as it is now. So why not let yourself go there?

Fear of disappointment, failure, and giving up is enough reason not to go there. When I look back at my own experience of meditating with thoughts of future becoming, one of the main reasons I would not follow such thoughts was the dread of coming out of one of these pleasant daydreams and feeling disappointed in my life—returning from a dream of having my ambition satisfied to a waking life of being nowhere near satisfying that ambition. So for many years in my meditation I would not entertain any pleasant fantasies about the future. I would tell myself that I didn't know what would happen in the future, so why bother wasting time imagining it? I wouldn't get what I wanted. I knew that because what I tended to want was something outside my ability to have: "It is not my karma." For a long time I thought I was free of such pleasant daydreams, but when I loosened my meditation practice and truly opened to these thoughts and fantasies, they rushed back in. And I am thankful that I have had the opportunity to sit with my ambitious thoughts and plans, for they have taught me more about what I need to be happy in my life than if I had kept them buried and silent.

Let me get more specific, with details from my life. Since I was a teenager I have had an ambition to be a successful novelist. I finished my first novel when I was twenty-six. Since I was living in Nepal at the time, I just showed it to some colleagues at work (who were English professors) and never sent it to a publisher. A couple of years later, I became involved in Vipassana meditation, and soon after that, I entered the Buddhist monastic order in Sri Lanka. My aspiration to be a novelist had no place in my life as a monk, so I didn't entertain any fantasies about it. Even when I left the monastic order, I was so committed to practicing and teaching meditation that I had no aspirations as a novelist. It wasn't until I decided not to see the pursuit to become a licensed psychotherapist to its conclusion, and consequently devote my life to teaching this approach to meditation, that the old ambition resurfaced.

I was out hiking one spring day in 1996 and couldn't stop ruminating about whether I should pursue writing a story that I was thinking about or just drop it. I didn't want to get into that mode of imagining characters and scenes and places and actions and a whole world of my own mental creation. I felt that it would take me away from working directly with people on their meditation practice. The question was either write fiction or teach meditation. I felt I couldn't do both at the same time. Whenever I thought of writing a novel, that teenage ambition would surface, with its grandiose fantasies and a strong feeling that the only way I would feel that my life was lived well would be by writing a great novel. And when I thought of teaching meditation, I felt compassion for the people I taught and wanted to do what I could to help them find their own path, their own independent practice. Each individual interview, each group reporting session, and every talk and retreat was serious work—I had to attend to what was going on in people's real lives. There was no glory in it. I had no big ambitions about teaching meditation. All I desired from the world was to be recognized and to have some financial security. Yet the grandiose novelist wanted popularity and eternal fame. He also wanted a lot of leisure time in order to write, and so I would have fantasies about writing instead of teaching. But I loved teaching, and still do, so the whole thing was quite confusing.

So on this walk, with all of this conflict going on inside me, I came to a decision. I would write fiction only if it served my meditation teaching (or dharma teaching). The aspiring novelist had to be subservient to the working meditation teacher. I felt that I had drawn up a contract in my mind that we both signed on the spot. I have had no confusion and no conflict regarding writing and teaching ever since. My novel writing became so much in the service of teaching that I would read sections of the novel I was working on as a bedtime story during a retreat. I have published a couple of my Buddhist novels (*King Bimbisara's Chronicler* and *Seeking Nibbana in Sri Lanka*) and have been gratified by hearing from people who have read them. And when I read one of them during a retreat, I am so happy that I spent so many unpaid days and exhausting hours writing them.

Here is the root of the struggle with thoughts of future becoming. Many of our hopes and desires for our future happiness may actually originate far in our past. In America, children are encouraged to dream about what they will become as adults. They get asked questions about what they would like to be when they grow up, and no doubt many of them remember how they answered those questions when they do grow up and find themselves living a totally different life. Then there are those times in your teens or early adulthood when you feel in your bones what it is you would like to do or what kind of person you would like to be. These feelings and the thoughts that go with them, can be very powerful in your life and may not fade or go away just because you have taken up meditation.

Going Into the Past

The past is perhaps the richest area of our experience on the cushion. As a teacher of Recollective Awareness, I value what the human memory can do. Of course there are ways in which memories limit, debilitate, and become unhealthily elaborated on. And there is always the criticism that remembered events can never be fully accurate, as our minds distort and color the past. But our minds do that in the present as well.

Here is the vantage point I intend to speak from: What has happened in the past is irreversible. The past cannot be changed. It is fixed and certain, and new information about it does not alter the facts, it just changes the story. Elaborations on the past are often ways we imagine things could have gone or should have gone, not how they happened. To see more deeply into the conditions of the past is often to face what has happened and come to an understanding of how it came to be. But people who are taught that all thinking is the same will make no distinction between such fanciful elaborations and skillful explorations.

What is the experience of going into the past like? You may be aware that your thoughts go into the past less often than into the future, though some meditation sittings may focus chiefly on the past. Certain emotions are more prone to bring us into the past, such as remorse and regret. Thoughts of what we said to certain people, or what they said to us, may occupy our minds in seemingly endless dialogues and monologues that will change nothing. When we try to look back into the past, it can sometimes be so blurry and so difficult to retrieve anything of substance that we wonder if it ever existed at all. But when the past erupts within us with unbidden images, feelings, and sense impressions, it seems all too real and is enough to swallow up the present.

Going Over Past Conversations

Going over past conversations in meditation can have a certain degree of redoing the conversation, having it all over again, except with some better comments on your part and a better outcome. These conversations can feel much the same as conversations you are intending to have in the future, and these two types of inner dialogue may trade off during a meditation sitting. What you should have said easily crosses over into what you will say. The past/future distinction, if applied, may obscure and distract you from what is actually going on in the present with these internal dialogues.

Say that at some time in your meditation sitting, you are talking to someone you work with. The other person had disagreed with you at your office about one of your ideas. You know your idea was a good one. You could not convince the other person of the merits of your idea at the time, so now you find yourself working on an argument outlining the highlights of your idea, but you are talking in your head to this person, presenting your arguments as you think of them. You are using this internal dialogue with this other person to help you work on and refine your idea. It may feel like you are arguing with him or trying to convince him at times—you may actually need to do that in order to see the flaws and assumptions in your idea. In a sense, you are bouncing your ideas off another person, counteracting that person's disagreement with better-formulated arguments, getting yourself to rethink something you thought was already thought out. When your thoughts go on like this, it is not about the past or the future, a real event or a fantasized one, or questions around why you are having this inner debate—it is a way to get your mind to think something through, going beyond where you would normally stop.

One can always reflect back on the internal dialogue described above and go into the emotions, views, and perceptions that keep them going. But here again, one may be trying to do that in order to stop or put the brakes on the onward flow of thoughts rather than being receptive to the thoughts and seeing where they lead. So if you are having a dialogue in which you disagree with someone and the thinking doesn't go in the direction of refining your argument but, rather, picks up steam in the direction of your being upset with the person, then being receptive to that emotion is what is called for.

FANCIFUL ELABORATION

There is also a great deal to be learned from reflecting back and becoming aware of ways you elaborate on the past. When you recall a period of your life that you are ashamed of, you would undoubtedly like to erase it and replace it with a less painful scenario. In meditation you may even give yourself the time to create such a scenario. It may even be quite believable, representing who you really are instead of that other person who did or said those regrettable things. Sometimes these scenarios extend into the future and spark you to do something about the past, but mostly they stay in a realm of imagining how you could have been instead of how you were.

Why would awareness of these replacement scenarios be useful? Could it be that this is also something you do in the present but can't quite see because you are in it? I mean, aren't we self-conscious beings who can't just leave flaws alone but have to do something about them? We would like to know what we did wrong and how to improve.

Many of us may be able to become aware of the awkward, hurtful, mistimed statement made to someone only after the fact, maybe not until someone else, or that person, brings it to our attention. The hurtful words sit there in the past, though they arise with a poignancy in the present. We think about them to correct them or to correct others' opinions about us or to become a more correct person.

So these elaborations aren't really harmful—they may even help you to avoid creating future harm. You may come up with a more skillful way of handling things next time, or better yet, you may truly see into the conditions that brought about the harmful action in the first place.

Memories Resurfacing

When following your thoughts and emotions in meditation, unwanted memories are bound to resurface. By allowing your thoughts to unfold, it is likely that a string of associations will form in your thinking and you will begin thinking about things you would rather not think about. Some of those thoughts might stir up difficult feelings. By staying with your feelings and not trying to direct them or redirect your attention away from them, you may also find yourself stumbling into emotions that you don't want to experience right now. This is often the case with traumatic memories.

When I was studying to become a psychotherapist, my first experience as a trainee was at a clinic for survivors of childhood sexual abuse and trauma. This was in the early nineties, when a lot of people were experiencing such memories and the therapeutic community was giving it a great deal of attention. I did not have that kind of experience in my childhood, so it was not easy for me to identify with the clients I saw. Around that time, the literature discussing why Freud switched from believing the stories of girls who reported having been abused by their parents to seeing them as fantasies was also gaining popularity. Sometimes the stories I was hearing sounded so true, and other times they were like dreams, and for a few people, they were complete fabrications. I had no way of knowing for sure. So when one of my clients would ask me to validate his or her story, I would have to come back with a basic statement of "If it feels true to you, then let's treat it as being true. If it doesn't feel like it really happened but you think it happened, then let's treat it as a possibility. And if it seems made up, then let's look further into how that came to be and what your memories are trying to tell you."

I saw many people getting too caught up in trying to find out whether they had been abused, as if that would answer many questions they had about why their life went in certain unfortunate directions. That question, "Why did my life go in this direction?" is a good one to ask regardless of whether there was something done to you in childhood. And if there was something done to you, that event may not explain everything, but it can explain some things. In meditation you might find that looking for a single explanation of why your life has turned out this way leads to some kind of conclusive narrative about your life. What if there is no single explanation?

Here we have the belief in a single cause leading to a specific effect. Maybe that cause, being some kind of trauma, for instance, is not the only reason that things have gone a certain way. It may just be a prominent (or dominant) condition and thus one of many conditions that were operating at the time. These lesser, secondary conditions are often ignored and disregarded when someone explores his or her past, especially if there is a story that sums it up. Allowing yourself to go back into past memories, when they arise naturally in your meditation sitting, may bring you to some awareness of conditions, or factors, that were present that you have been largely unaware of.

I recall a student many years ago who looked at a particular childhood trauma in his meditation. It wasn't sexual. His father punished him by burning all of his books, and he was an avid reader. This student has done a great deal of therapeutic work around the trauma itself. His meditation sittings, however, brought up additional memories about where he lived at the time, his relationship with his parents, what it was like being that age, and what reading meant to him, to name some of what he recalled. This process did not cure the trauma, as this kind of meditation may be helpful only for sitting with and exploring traumatic memories, not necessarily for working through them.

One thing that this meditation practice will do is help you tolerate the feelings better, be kinder to yourself when you have such memories, and become more willing and able to explore the various and many conditions surrounding the trauma.

Nostalgia, Reminiscing

Since serious meditators are not supposed to get attached to pleasant experiences, many Vipassana meditators curtail their reveries in their meditation sittings. One kind of reverie is going into the past and dwelling in a pleasurable memory. It may be hard to tear yourself away from recalling a beautiful place you visited, a warm and lovely encounter with another person, or the pleasure of a certain accomplishment. These kinds of memories will most likely surface on their own in meditation, and you can always choose to let them go on unimpeded. There are things to be learned from such memories.

Simply, what we have enjoyed in the past, we most likely want to enjoy again in the future. These pleasant scenes and feelings from the past are active in us and are informing our choices, even on the most basic level of what we want to eat, drink, see, and do. We live to repeat past pleasures, even though we may look for them in different forms (that tricky notion that the new one or next time will be more pleasurable). By meditating with your de-lightful memories, you may start to pick up how they became pleasant and attractive and why you feel a need to spend time and money and energy pursuing them.

I am not saying, however, that by doing this you will become free from pursuing those pleasures. With pleasures and desires, I don't believe there is a single way to get free of them. I mean that if you want to loosen the hold these pleasant memories have over you, you first have to be willing to renounce a pleasure and the accompanying desire for it. So as long as you are still committed to having pleasure in your life, you are not seeking the end of all sense pleasures. Perhaps you just don't want to be controlled by them. If that is the case, there should be no problem with allowing pleasant memories and reveries to go on in your meditation sit-tings. But you may find that some pleasures just aren't worth it anymore. You may notice that you have outgrown certain plea-sures. And you may question whether certain pleasures are really that good for you. This type of assessment of pleasures in your life can be furthered by meditation sittings where such memories are followed and even enjoyed.

Along these lines are those memories that we need to have in order to feel positive about our life. Remembering some work well done, a good deed, a charitable act, a creative and thoughtful project, a deeply moving meditation sitting, can inject you with a feeling of well-being and give you needed encouragement. I have encountered many meditators who have only painful memories or who focus only on the unpleasant ones and thus have difficulty noticing and staying with positive and self-affirming memories. For those folks, differentiating a positive memory from the rest of their thinking is important. Only by doing that can its value be recognized.

REPETITION

We may read about the wheel of existence, the theory of renewed existence, the rearising of certain tendencies and habits, the con-ditioning and patterning of our experience, so why does it seem so difficult at times to tolerate repetitive thoughts in meditation? What is so painful about going over a conversation you had prior to sitting? Is it the topic? Or is it that it keeps repeating itself, seemingly to torment you?

My sense is that we often delude ourselves into believing that an interaction with someone won't come back to haunt us, that our actions won't return to us like a boomerang, and that what we think about won't crop up in our thought stream again once we've determined we are done with it. Take away the delusion and you will find that it is an entirely normal and common affair to experience a recurrence of thoughts and emotions from things you have perceived, thought, said, and done. Our past has to come back. We can't just sever ourselves from it.

In meditation we are perhaps more vulnerable to repressed memories, rehashed conversations, relived situations, especially in an open, unstructured practice such as Recollective Awareness meditation. Knowing that memories will flow into your meditation sitting and that you may find yourself pursuing them is different from believing that once you sit down to meditation you are going to open up only to new experiences. As you become more willing to let memories flow, old behaviors resurface, and habitual patterns of thinking emerge, you may find that you can find them interesting, educational, worthy of further exploration. Instead of turning away from repetition or trying to turn it off, you may find that by going through it again and again you actually do move into some new, unfamiliar experiences.

So whenever I hear from a student that she is tired of having the same old thoughts, of going through the same psychological issues, of reliving events that are far in the past and have little or no bearing on what is going on today, I inquire as to how she has been relating to those experiences. If she notices a positive change in how she relates to those thoughts and feelings, even though they haven't really subsided or gone away, then something significant is happening in her meditation practice: repetition is becoming tolerated and may even be accepted as being necessary for some useful learning to occur.

When something that has come up repeatedly has stopped, then you know that it has changed for you. Those who have not been open to repetition in their meditation practice may find it harder to know when the fuel has withdrawn from a particular behavior, habit, view, or craving. This goes back to the Buddha's *sutta* to Vacchagotta on facing the fire in front of him. By letting the fire burn, thus allowing repetitive thoughts and emotions, you can see into it and discover what fuels it, but if you douse the fire with water, putting it out prematurely, you learn nothing about repetition—all you have found is a strategy to suppress it temporarily.

It is in this area of repeating thoughts and emotions that the past, present, and future seem to come together for us. Such thoughts and emotions, which surely make up a majority of our inner experience, are a bit different when they occupy each of these time periods. Thoughts and emotions in the past seem to be over; in the present they fill our minds; and those that pertain to the future fuel our daydreams, desires, grievances, and ambitions. When we train our minds in meditation to become aware of thoughts and emotions, we learn how the past enters into our experience of the present and how the present moment may influence the future.

8

Higher Values in Meditation

There was a time when the purpose of meditation was very simple for me. It was about eliminating defilements, seeing things as they are, and becoming fully liberated, which are all part and parcel of the same thing: awakening (*nibbana*). Meditation practices that did not purport to lead to such an awakening didn't interest me. They were for other people. Such techniques might lead to stress reduction, relaxation, or trance states, but they were inferior because they did not teach a direct path to liberation. As I write this, I am filled with a fair amount of shame at what an arrogant person I was back then.

But not all people who hold the belief that meditation is to be done solely in the service of awakening are arrogant. The trouble with me as a young man was that, when I was entirely honest with myself, treating awakening or enlightenment as the highest value was just not congruent with the other values I had been operating with. For along with the overvaluing of enlightenment came other values that I was less comfortable with: leaving the world (which I tried to do as a monk), not becoming attached to people (not having dear friendships and meaningful long-term relationships), being totally obedient to an authority figure and accepting everything he said without question (giving myself over to my teacher), and following rules of conduct and behavior to the letter without being able to consider the implications of the rules and behaviors. This is some of what one takes on when striving for awakening in Theravada Buddhism.

If I had grown up believing that these values led to a happy and fulfilled life, I might not have struggled so hard with them, having to discipline myself to get in step with these values. I felt that my progressive success at doing what it took to become awakened was some kind of great accomplishment. And that was how I could become arrogant about it—if it had been easy for me to leave the world, submit to authority, obey rules to the letter, and become unattached to friends, then it would just be natural and there would be nothing to be proud about. I had to go against my own nature to make these values work for me, applying a good deal of effort to make that happen, and so, of course, I would build a self around it.

What eventually happened is that I had to thoroughly question the value at the top: awakening. Once that was questioned as the sole purpose and benefit of meditation, I could then question the values that others had presented to me as essential for awakening. Over the years, I have whittled away the notions of awakening from my meditation practice and teaching and, in the process, have gained a greater understanding of what awakening is about. To me it has to do with another set of values, ones that I am more comfortable with and can endorse. Though, oddly enough, after having been a Theravada Buddhist monk, it took me some time to fully reembrace some of the values I had left behind.

The first value that I struggled to reincorporate into my life after I left the monastic order was that of forming enduring relationships with people. I was in the world now, and being in the world meant talking at meals, working at a job, seeing a therapist, training to be a therapist, being in a committed marriage, and so forth. I remember my psychology teachers, and the therapists who supervised me, presenting me with the view that a meaningful life was to be found in one's relationships with others. It wasn't about awakening, which they mostly had no understanding of, but about something quite inferior in the eyes of those that seek enlightenment: having satisfying relationships with one's partner, friends, colleagues, and even one's parents and siblings. But I also saw looking into my interpersonal relationships as work I had put off during my years in robes, so I went into it with an open mind. It also made sense. Now that I was living with my wife, lived near my parents (who were divorced), and was in the world as an ordinary person, I had to recover this valuing of human relationships. In time, not only did I learn to value each and every relationship I was in, but I also came to see how meditation practice can help people look at their relationships instead of being one of the ways to escape them.

Even though I was no longer a monk, I still observed my behavior and conduct as though I were. I kept aloof at parties and social gatherings (which I begrudgingly attended, mostly for my mother's or father's sake). I was very careful about my speech and would be quiet in many conversations owing to my reluctance to talk about certain subjects. When I stayed with people, they would get annoyed by my always asking for permission to use their things, as I wanted to be sure I would never be accused of taking something that was not given. And one day I went to lunch with a friend at a seafood restaurant and turned down lobster because it had to be killed on the spot for me to eat it. It was as if I felt an obligation to hold to whatever monastic rules I could as a layperson. But then I got to see some of the negative consequences of my following some of these rules, which was harder to see when I was a monk. This rule-following behavior made me so much more self-occupied and self-conscious than I would normally be, and this was not a desirable condition in the least. It crippled my communication with most people, got in the way of my having a good time in the company of others, and precipitated hours of guilt for doing minor and inconsequential acts.

Being unable to live as a strict follower of rules forced me to find some other way to assess good and right behavior. My training in psychotherapy was helping me in this. Hearing others reflect on their past actions with a willingness to explore them gave me more trust in the process of learning about what is good and right from looking closely at the motivations behind actions. So much of our behavior is unexamined. Meditation can help one go back over past actions, in complete privacy and trust, and see more clearly what was going on that contributed to those actions. This led to valuing a practice of reflecting back on and internally processing questionable actions as a way to correct future behavior.

My obedience to authority was actually the hardest to address and took the most time and mental energy. I felt that I was mostly in agreement with the Buddha and that others had misunderstood his teaching and were thus in disagreement with me, though they felt they were in agreement with the Buddha. More than twenty years later, there are more and more people who are in this predicament regarding the Buddha's teaching, so my early rebellion against the commentarial interpretations of the Buddha's discourses is far more commonplace. This has given me a bird's-eye view of my own situation that I didn't have at the time, when I thought I was one of the only people asking certain questions and getting into particular debates. When you are in a debate, you think there is a right point of view, a winning argument, and it is all settled. From my current vantage point, we have to choose our authority. And here I recovered a value that I really had neglected during the time when I was a monk, even though conceptually it was considered an integral part of the meditation practice: listening to the truth of each person's experience. Someone else cannot know more of what is going on in your mind than you do yourself. But it is my task to get to know another's inner world as well as I can, especially if I am that person's meditation teacher. And along with that is the acceptance that what another person says is the truth of her experience—even when it goes against my notion of the truth of someone's experience, it is her truth. So if someone tells me she had a conversation with God in her meditation sitting, instead of being a disbelieving and disapproving authority, I am interested in hearing about her experience. In the same way, if someone talks to me about a past-life memory, I treat that as true and meaningful to that person and make no judgment about it, leaving it up to the person to find the truth of it for herself.

After being a meditation teacher for the past twenty-five years, I find that the questions surrounding authority never go away. What makes me an authority and not someone else? Well, in truth, I am an authority for only a small patch of ground known as Recollective Awareness meditation. Some of us Western Buddhist teachers have been accused of niche marketing, but I think it is more of an organic process than a consumer-driven one. I, for instance, started out teaching the Mahasi method as it was taught to me in Sri Lanka, but I found it was not entirely to my style or my liking, and so I conscientiously worked on developing my own approach to Vipassana meditation. Other Vipassana teachers have done something similar, or they have stuck to teaching the meditation practices they learned from their teachers. Here is where many people place the authority issue: Only those who faithfully teach the traditional methods are recognized as legitimate. They have greater authority in the establishment than we innovators. But they have no idea how to teach Recollective Awareness meditation, so how could they be authorities in regard to this practice?

In order to get to this point, I had to value the meditation practice I developed as being suitable for some people but not for everyone. It is certainly not the only way to meditate, nor is it the best way for everyone to meditate. It is just a good way for some people to meditate. And it doesn't hurt to try it out.

Healthy Skepticism

Doubting, rather than denying, metaphysical beliefs and dogmatic assertions that do not fit your experience is what most skepticism is about. I would extend that doubt to the beliefs that are part of a meditation practice. The problem most people have with doubting the meditation practice they are doing is that it works best when you don't doubt it.

Doubting a belief you have about yourself or that someone else has about you is a type of skepticism. You may hold on to certain beliefs about yourself as tightly as a religious fundamentalist holds to his dogma. You may have certain narratives about your life that have never been examined, that you have not had the least trace of doubt about, because they seem absolutely true. And they may well seem true because they are apparently based on facts. But when it comes to your life, what are *facts*?

A fact seems to be an unchanging truth. It is what would appear in your biodata, on your medical records, in your file, and eventually, in your obituary. But these facts leave the stories behind them untold. They are tied to social conventions and what people in positions of authority and power deem as relevant information about you. They are thus skewed away from the personal; they rarely touch what you know about yourself and those close to you know about you from living with you. As you move into seeing your world as made up of thoughts, sensations, emotions, and various states of mind, such facts as found in your résumé do not tell the whole story of what you are experiencing; in fact, they may be mostly irrelevant regarding your experience.

Any prolonged meditation practice will chip away at what you have taken up as an identity, and so will many forms of serious long-term psychotherapy. I believe that is mostly because of your narratives' being up for discussion during a time when a greater connection and appreciation of your inner world is developing. For one who doesn't have a connection with one's inner world, all there is to define oneself is the connection with one's family, friends, groups, communities, nation, and so on. Those who already have a connection with their inner world before taking up meditation often feel as if they were coming home when they start meditating. Meditating is a way of remembering our internal life and seeing it as just as vital as the life we have in society, if not more so. And sometimes we are surprised at how much other people value a healthy and well-developed inner life in someone. But we do need to cultivate a sense of the importance of our inner world in order to question what the outer world has gotten us to believe as unchanging truths about ourselves.

Are there inner *facts*? If you treat each thought, emotion, or sensation as an unchanging truth, then you are not being faithful to your experience. For instance, if you experience a few minutes of truly hating someone, that doesn't mean that you hate that person—all it means is that you have experienced a few minutes of hating that person and that hating someone can be a fleeting experience as long as you don't turn it into a story of how from now on you will always hate that person. It is when the hate for that individual keeps recurring and seems to be a "fact" of your life that the stories you believe become an unchanging truth. But how can a temporary feeling be deemed a permanent reality? What gives it that illusion?

Lack of skill regarding how your inner world operates gives it that illusion. You may not be able to question how you turned a recurring feeling into a belief of how you feel all the time. You have probably put more time and energy into building the narrative that you feel this way all the time about this person than into turning your attention to exploring how this feeling and the beliefs based on it operate. I believe one of the reasons we build such narratives is that we are not skeptical about the validity of such stories. If you could be skeptical of the fact that you hate somebody unconditionally all the time, then you might find enough evidence to support a narrative that you hate the person only conditionally, that is, when he says or does certain things. At other times, such as when he is nice and friendly, hatred for him doesn't arise. But that may feel too confusing. You sometimes hate him and are sometimes fond of him. You may have quite a variety of feelings that come up at different times around him, but instead of seeing these feelings as coming about through conditions, you tend to default back to allowing only one of the feelings to define what you feel about this person and discounting the rest. This is not a skillful way to work with confusion, though it may seem to get the desired result of ending the confusion and coming to a conclusion.

Following this path of skepticism is the process of getting more familiar with your confusion and not disregarding it as a distraction, an impediment, or a sign of failure. Confusion is a painful emotion and can be just as debilitating as grief or sadness. Most meditation practices and teachings shield the student from becoming confused by giving the student dogmatic or systematic instructions, views, and answers to questions. The basic myth here is that there should be no doubt in the student's mind as long as she is doing the instructions correctly and paying attention to the teachings she is given. Doubt, as the story often goes, comes about from thinking too much and not doing the instructions right and not paying attention. And those who doubt too much (or too often) are left to their own devices—they will never get what everyone gets who follows the straight path that is being taught.

So Recollective Awareness is a meditation practice for those who doubt too much with too great a frequency, and it lines up with a meditation practice for those who think too much and have strong emotions in meditation. Here is a practice where confusion is a sign of progress, not failure. You just have to be willing to sit with your confusion.

This is an easy meditation practice to doubt. It is perfect for doubters. The instruction to allow your thoughts and emotions into your meditation sitting goes against the grain of so many teachings on meditation that you must doubt it at some level. I mean, the instruction to be aware of the breath makes so much immediate sense. No one questions it. When it is stated that awareness of breath will lead to elimination of stress, freedom from desire, and even enlightenment, people think of proving those outcomes rather than doubting them. The logic is clear: the most meditative-sounding instructions will lead to the implied goals of meditation, while the least meditative-sounding instructions won't get you even close.

Since letting thoughts and emotions run on and on in your meditation sitting doesn't sound like meditation, you can easily doubt that it can take you to the same places as other meditation practices—that is, until you see for yourself that it has. And hopefully that experience of seeing where this meditation practice leads can counteract this doubt to the degree that your doubts don't stop you from meditating in this way.

When it is just your own personal meditation practice, over-coming your doubts about it is an individual matter. But you might feel alone doing this kind of meditation while others are doing more traditional or "evidence-based" meditation practices where there is no room for doubt. You might feel that because your meditation practice is hard to explain and easy to dismiss, others are not going to take it seriously, that you are always going to have to defend it or not say any more about it. You may feel it is even proper and appropriate to take other people's doubts about this practice on board and validate them, and while doing so be-tray your own hard-won knowledge about meditation and trade it for someone else's right-sounding technique.

As I said, doubting is part of this practice. And doubting this practice while doing it, especially at times when there really is something to question about it, is a key feature of this practice. But the difference between doubting this practice while at the same time sticking with it and having little or no confidence in it is huge.

In the first few weeks or months and sometimes years of prac-ticing this approach to meditation, it is quite natural for certain questions to arise. These questions often come with doubts and confusion about this practice, and I certainly wouldn't want to disrupt your internal process of doubting this teaching by giving some instruction or advice that would lead to avoiding the doubt. Many doubts about this practice can be examined through a rec-ognition of certain higher values found in the meditation prac-tices one has heard about or been taught. So instead of looking at a change in the meditation instructions, I will first look at shifting to a different, higher value, one which could open up questioning beliefs inherited from another meditation practice. For instance, someone poses a question regarding the use of effort in medita-tion practice. This question comes from a belief in accomplishing things through hard work, pain, and discipline. In the questioner's mind, persistent and focused effort is the higher value. So I might offer the possibility that his overvaluing of effort may be the source of his doubt and confusion about this approach. Then I would suggest that he consider other higher values, such as kindness, tolerance, patience, self-honesty, and wholeness, for that may temper some of his doubt and reduce some of his confusion. He doesn't have to give up his belief in effort; he is asked only to place that value alongside other higher values and observe his meditation practice from that alternative perspective.

As you read through the following three vignettes, you might find that some of my suggestions may actually produce more doubt. Part of the reason you might be asking doubting questions in the first place is that you may be seeing this practice as the same, in certain respects, as the other practices you have done in the past. But this isn't like those other practices in one key respect—it really may not get any clearer or more orderly as you continue. Only you can give answers to your questions regarding this approach; all I can do in this book is give you some suggestions regarding choices you can make in your meditation sittings when certain questions arise in your practice. But remember, when you follow a suggestion and don't believe in the value it is based on, then it may turn out to be frustrating and counterproductive, so if you have a conflict with the values inherent in the suggestion, you would probably be better off sitting with the internal conflict rather than doing what I suggest. Alternately, you might as well ignore the suggestion and just sit as you would normally.

Vignette 1

Once you allow thinking into your meditation practice, you open the door for drifting off in meditation as well. Even though people can get tired and sleepy doing any kind of meditation practice, there is usually an orientation toward trying to wake yourself up when you find yourself slipping off to sleep. This might not be so bad when there is a ready explanation for being tired, but when it seems to happen in practically each and every sitting, apparently coming out of nowhere, then you might wonder if you will ever get this meditation thing right.

In this instance, I am reminded of a woman who contacted me

after reading *Unlearning Meditation*, having found this practice of being gentle with and allowing your thoughts and emotions to be what she was looking for. But it wasn't a natural fit for her. She had already done about two decades of Insight meditation, mostly at the Insight Meditation Society at Barre, Massachusetts, and had successfully developed a meditation practice of bringing her attention back to her breath whenever her mind wandered. Her Insight meditation practice was layered on top of conditioning as a child to always pay attention in school, never be idle, and always do things that have a purpose—sitting in meditation had to be productive and could never be wasteful. Drifting off, or God forbid, falling asleep, was to be prevented at all costs.

Her first year of doing Recollective Awareness meditation was filled with compromises between this approach and traditional Insight meditation, as I would expect. She would allow more thinking and permit it to go on longer, but she would feel compelled to try to notice each time she had a thought and what it was about. Many people who transition into this type of meditation practice from a noting practice such as Insight meditation or mindfulness meditation tend to put more effort into trying to remember their thoughts in the meditation sitting. They won't just let themselves think about something in meditation—they have to notice it and recall it, using Recollective Awareness in much the same way as present-moment awareness. So they end up with sittings that have this kind of scenario:

I kept noticing how I'd be present, set an intention to see what was occurring, and the next time I was aware was when I came to in a particular thought. Then I would name that thought, which would stop that thought. A few moments later I would be in another thought, and this whole process would start again. At the end of the meditation sitting, I could recall only a few of the thoughts I named. Not the actual thoughts, however, just the names I used when I became aware of them.

For people coming out of a mindfulness practice, to be aware is synonymous with being awake. If they can't just let thoughts go on and resist the tendency to stop and label each one, then how much harder is it going to be to let themselves drift toward sleep and wake up not remembering a thing? So the first suggestion I often give in this situation, especially if someone has done a mindfulness practice, is to stop trying to recollect your experiences, for it is often being done as a noting practice and not as a Recollective Awareness practice. The distinction here is that a Recollective Awareness practice allows the thinking to go on and on, bringing in awareness after the thinking has gone on for some time as well as after the meditation is over. And with Recollective Awareness, one may recall very little, but what one does recall is not the label given to the experience, as in a noting practice, but the fuller experience, which can be described in a fresh, new way.

At this point, there needs to be a shift from one set of values to another. The first set of values has to do with being awake and aware all of the time. My suggestion is to value the capacity to be receptive to, and tolerant of, your full range of thoughts and emotions in meditation. I see this also as valuing a broad awareness of one's inner experiences and states of mind, not just the ones we put our attention on. In this situation, awareness cannot be equated with being awake; it must be defined differently *as the level of awareness that is present with the experience one is having.* If one is sleepy, then the level of awareness is affected by being sleepy; you cannot become aware of what sleepiness is like by waking up—you have enough awareness while you feel sleepy to register what that experience is like.

Allowing thinking to go on in meditation will lead to allowing drifting off, to being drawn into emotions and fantasies, and will generally open the door for any kind of experience one can have while sitting. The value of this kind of opening up to the full range of your inner world has be acknowledged to some degree in your meditation practice in order to keep meditating this way. If you don't, then surely you will doubt it on the very grounds that you tend to spend a lot of time thinking about useless things, going into sleepy states that seem worthless, and having to deal with feelings and memories that seem intrusive and unnecessary.

But what happens when you meditate with two conflicting values, such as being both aware/awake and receptive/tolerant? You may go back and forth between the two practices, doing them at different times, or you may struggle to find a compromise. Many people who transition from mindfulness practice to Recollective Awareness meditation have to make some kind of compromise in order to keep doing this. At first the openness and allowing is only partial. There are still many trains of thought that are not really allowed, some of which the person isn't aware of because they end prematurely. And then there are things they were warned against in meditation—never to let themselves slouch, drool, lean forward on their cushion, and so on—for that would be a public display of falling asleep in meditation and would, in many circles, be taken as an indication that one is a bad meditator.

I would suggest that you let yourself do the things that have been seen as a sign of failure. You are not doing them intentionally—there is no decision to fall asleep during meditation; in fact, your intention is probably quite the contrary. So falling asleep or drifting off in meditation is not your fault, and it certainly does not say anything about your skillfulness and promise as a meditator. I often say that it is a good idea to know what sleep is really like in meditation so that you can distinguish it from other states of mind that seem like sleep but really aren't, and the only way for that to happen is to let yourself fall asleep in meditation.

The resistance many people have to this invitation arises from the fear that when they meditate in public they might snore. True enough, snoring in the meditation hall can be disruptive for some people, but it can also be instructive. What makes someone else's snoring so intolerable? If I can't stop it from happening, how can I learn to be with it?

This leads to my next suggestion: meditation is about being with the existing conditions in your experience, and falling asleep, or someone else's snoring, is an existing condition. Be more open to the conditions that are arising and manifesting at the moment instead of trying to get things to be a certain way. I'm not asking you to be present, awake, or clear, just open, kind, gentle, allowing.

This is a different set of values. Instead of valuing effort, you value patience and kindness.

Here the underlying tendency most meditators have in this regard can be addressed: the drive toward productivity. Meditation cannot be equated with sitting around doing nothing in the minds of some people. It has to be work. Otherwise it is not a legitimate use of one's time. So meditation instructions involve "work." Doing the instructions correctly is considered being productive, even when it doesn't yield the promised result. At least you are doing something while sitting in meditation and not just spacing out.

The notion that meditation has to be productive most of the time, or produce immediate results, is a value that needs to be examined in order to feel comfortable practicing Recollective Awareness meditation. This value is truly antithetical to the project of sitting in meditation, regardless of the tradition. It is one of the reasons many people give up on meditation—they can't be productive meditators and don't get immediate results. You don't have to be productive in each meditation sitting, or in each and every moment of your experience, in order for meditation to have a welcomed effect on your life. It is not about being productive while meditating but, rather, the effects your meditation sittings have on your well-being, your decisions, your relationships, and your work. And allowing yourself to drift off in meditation, if you become okay with it, may actually have a good effect on your overall well-being. It may be just what you need at that time. You may find yourself coming out of such a meditation sitting feeling refreshed and ready to work. You may also experience less stress and less self-criticism about drifting off in meditation if you willingly allow it and treat it as something that happens to everyone who meditates, whether they like it or not.

This doesn't mean your meditation sittings will always feel unproductive. There often comes a time when more "work" is occurring in the sitting and your sittings resemble what you may have found in other practices. There are many examples of this happening on retreat and in people's meditation journals. But to get to a place where the sittings begin to feel productive, you may have to temporarily give up on their being so.

Vignette 2

Sitting down to meditate and having a slew of thoughts rush into your head and then doing nothing about it when you know you could settle your mind a bit first may seem crazy and unreasonable. What is the advantage of letting thoughts and emotions build and consume you at the beginning of a meditation sitting? Why not first calm your mind with a practice of following the breath, using a mantra, reciting some phrases, or any other means by which you can get settled?

Over the years I have met several people who have had difficulty with Recollective Awareness meditation precisely because of this point. Often they do not stick it out to see where sitting with all of this chaotic inner conflict and intensity could lead. The reasoning goes, *If I can get myself into a calm and equanimous state of mind at the beginning of a meditation sitting, then I could observe my thoughts and emotions without getting caught up in them. And along with being a calm observing witness to my experience, I would also find that the thoughts and emotions vanish and leave me with a clear mind to be aware of the breath or body sensations.* And some people take this even further, adding, *This experience of stillness and detachment in the observing consciousness is the way I would like to be all of the time.*

You can see that it would be futile for me to try to convince someone with this kind of experience that it would be in his best interest to meet the chaos in his mind instead of following the routine of intentionally calming his mind. Even as I write this, I know it is a hard sell.

So let me approach this divergent view around practice in terms of values. The higher value of a clear and equanimous observing consciousness dominates a good deal of meditation practice. It may even be taught as the goal of meditation. Whenever such a luminous consciousness arises, it is excellent. It has the status of an optimal state of consciousness. But here is where we could be a bit more discerning. It may not be the optimal state of consciousness with which to explore your thoughts and emotions, simply because it wants to have nothing to do with them. It is a state of mind that is often incapable of actually being interested in thoughts and emotions. Besides that, it can rarely, if ever, know an emotion at its actual intensity because it mutes and diminishes such emotions, and the same goes for thoughts, which seldom last when you are in an optimal equanimous state of mind. If we just take this optimal state of mind for what it is, for however long it lasts, and look at as we would any other state of mind, we may find what it is actually good for, what it actually does, and then we can make a more accurate assessment of its value. But people rarely ever do that kind of investigation, because such states of mind are often considered sacred, privileged, special.

Having done that type of investigation on numerous occasions and having read and listened to the meditation reports of others who have done the same, I find that calm and equanimous states of mind may actually be good for developing *samadhi* rather than insight. That is, it may make much more sense to let such optimal states move toward becoming more inward, more removed, quieter and stiller, and not burden them with the task of observing thoughts and emotions. Let such states produce their own state-dependent objects of awareness, such as colors, images, scenes, sounds, perceptions of space, and so forth. What I am suggesting is that you let yourself go into them and let them carry you away. There is no need to use them to scrutinize your experience; that is for a different kind of calm state of mind, one that is more practically developed out of a practice of staying with the chaotic inner conflict and intensity that you may find when you sit with thoughts and emotions as they naturally reveal themselves to your awareness.

The shift in values I am recommending here is that you value your capacity to be with and tolerate your thoughts and emotions in meditation over your capacity to detach from them. So if someone has a tendency to detach quickly from feelings and enter into a calm state of mind at the beginning of his sittings, a corrective instruction would be in order. But you may doubt this instruction, struggle with it, or just not bother with it. It will go against the grain of your practice and will contradict the higher value of calmness, equanimity, and peace you have had for meditation. What I suggest is simply that when you sit down to meditate, let whatever you were thinking about or feeling before the sitting directly into the meditation. Do not do any preparatory or opening practice in the sitting— even taking refuge or doing a short invocation or chant can interfere with your attempt to start a sitting with your mind as it was before the sitting. In this way, the boundary between what your mind is like before a meditation sitting and what it is like in a meditation sitting gets dissolved. What most people don't like about this approach is that their mind in meditation then becomes more like their mind outside of meditation, which for experienced meditators may feel like going backward.

Vignette 3

Rarely do I hear from students the notion of thinking good thoughts as a way to get rid of bad thoughts, since people who wholeheartedly believe in positive thinking are unlikely to be drawn to this kind of meditation. But I do hear the idea that practicing good, wholesome thoughts, when done consistently over time, will create a mental habit of thinking good thoughts, and so, the reasoning tends to go, the time you spend thinking of good, positive things will outweigh the times you think of negative things. Also, from the preponderance of wholesome thoughts will arise more occasions of wholesome speech and action. Essentially, by thinking compassionate thoughts and doing meditation practices for that purpose, you will find compassion to be more readily accessible, more a part of your daily interactions, more of who you are.

So the doubt about Recollective Awareness becomes *Why allow negative thoughts to dominate? Doesn't that just produce more negative thinking? How can that lead to good, wholesome thoughts and actions?*

For these questions to be answered satisfactorily, the higher values would need to shift from goodness to authenticity, self-honesty, and humility. In Recollective Awareness meditation we are working toward becoming aware, wise, and compassionate individuals, not just good, positive-thinking people. We are not going to compromise our awareness practice to censor our experience and promote only the thoughts we want. So instead we move toward being honest with ourselves when we feel hatred, envy, lust, greed, and other negative emotions. We don't want to replace them each time they arise—that would not be honest. Instead, we are learning how to be kind and interested in these negative emotions—knowing that we are ignorant about them—so that some kind of wisdom can form out of our experience of being with them. This whole process is humbling, for we cannot rest in the conceit of being such a good and wonderful person when our honest awareness of ourselves tells us otherwise.

This doesn't mean seeing yourself as fatally flawed from birth. That narrative can have just as much conceit as seeing yourself as perfect from birth. This is about being aware of your good qualities and your bad ones, your shining talents and your imperfections, and those aspects of yourself that fit between, or outside, the categories of good and bad.

That is where the practice of Recollective Awareness meditation will take you. You may find it confusing to sit with ill will, for example, and be utterly calm and understanding with yourself for feeling that way. In the past you may have had to get rid of the hatred in your heart whenever it flared up, but now you stay with it and find you don't really want to act on it, but it pushes you to do so. This hatred is negative, it is not the way you want to be seen, but here it is, and only you are knowing that you are that way as you sit in meditation. This is the kind of self-honesty that supports this meditation practice.

How does this lead to the cultivation of good qualities? You may doubt that sitting with hatred could ever lead to compassion, but how do you know it won't? To do so, you may need to trust your mind more. You may need to remember how in sittings past you were able to move from hatred to kindness, from desire to contentment, and from delusion to more clarity. Your mind will move toward the positive if that is your overall intention in life. Instead of trying to micromanage your thoughts and emotions, trying to get from negative to positive states in the blink of an eye, let the process be a longer one, a more authentic, human struggle, trusting that your mind will gradually gravitate toward the qualities you are trying to cultivate and away from the ones you have had enough of in your life.

A woman came to one of my retreats with a practice of meditating with both hands on her heart, generating loving feelings for herself. In the first interview we had, she talked about how she did this at the beginning of each sitting and that it enabled her to get to a place of happiness, self-acceptance, and serenity. I wasn't about to say that there was something wrong in that. All I did was suggest that she try beginning her sittings by being gentle to herself but without the technique of holding her hands over her heart.

At first there was little change in her meditation sittings, perhaps because she was doing much the same thing as before, except without using her hands. But then, as she listened to my talks and to the reports of other meditators on their sittings, she got the idea of just sitting with whatever comes up and decided on her own to allow more of her thoughts and emotions into her sittings. After going through a storm or two and coming out with greater calm, ease, self-compassion, and understanding for herself, she became more trusting of this process. At the end of the retreat she remarked that this practice had brought about the kind of self-honesty and authenticity she was looking for.

9

A Theory of Awareness

It is helpful to have a theory of awareness that works for learning more about your subjective inner experience. These days such a theory would need to be corroborated by research done in the field of neuroscience. I am not talking about a theory on how the mind/brain really works but, rather, on one primary function of the human mind: awareness. Granted, there can be more than one competing theory on the nature of awareness, for that is indeed the case. What I am doing is choosing one that I believe can be of value when applied to an open meditation practice.

This theory is not entirely my own. It is taken from readings in cognitive science, neuroscience, Western psychology and philosophy, and Buddhist psychology and philosophy. My trust in it comes from how I and those whom I have taught have applied it to our understanding of how awareness works in Recollective Awareness meditation practice.

Awareness, as I see it, is a flexible, malleable mental faculty. How it functions is dependent on the state of mind you are in. When you are sleepy, your awareness will probably have a sluggish, dull quality to it, and on account of that, you might not remember much afterward. When you are bright and alert, your awareness may have a clear and quick quality, and your capacity to recall what you were aware of may be quite good. Much of the day you are probably functioning somewhere between bright/alert and sleepy/dull, and your awareness is sufficient to get you through the familiar things that arise. If you put effort into recalling things that you or other people have said during the day, or what you saw, heard, smelled, tasted, touched, and thought, then you might notice that you can recall some parts of the day quite easily but not other things.

This scenario applies to your meditation sittings as well. When you write down your meditation experiences afterward in your journal, some parts of the sitting are clear, while others are hazy, and yet others are completely forgotten. There is no constant level of awareness throughout a meditation sitting, and this is not a failure on your part—it is just the way it is. Trying to change this situation by becoming mindful of each moment of your experience, as taught in mindfulness meditation, does not acknowledge that a fluctuating awareness is of use. Instead, the mindfulness theory of awareness seeks to create a higher-level awareness that is constant, and thus it discounts periods of your awareness that are dull and unclear.

The usefulness of a fluctuating awareness is that it enables us to become aware of the full range of conscious experience after the fact. It enables us to remember dreams, hypnagogic states, trance states, drugged states, and what it is like when we emerge from a state of mind where there was no awareness, such as deep sleep. It also helps us when we would like to recall what else was going on when we were feeling a certain way or had a certain encounter or said something to somebody. That is, it may help us when we try to recollect something that may have been going on in the background of our experience that we were dimly aware of but not focusing on.

Such subtleties of experience may not be noticed while they are going on. Daniel Stern, in his book *The Present Moment in Psychotherapy and Everyday Life,* describes what he calls a microanalytic interview that he has done with patients for many years. He asks a patient to talk about what she experienced that morning at breakfast. At first she might not recall much. Then he asks her more direct questions regarding the details of certain actions, such as pouring a cup of tea, and what went on while she was pouring the tea. Once he ascertains an action that has a definite beginning and end point, like pouring a cup of tea, he asks minute questions about what the patient "did, thought, felt, saw, heard, what position their body was in, when it shifted, whether they positioned themselves as an actor or an observer to the action, or somewhere in between." He wouldn't stop there but would go on to create on a blackboard diagram of all that happened within that short span of time, taking the patient through the experience over and over again, drawing up new details, connections, and associations in the process. He writes, "Continuities and discontinuities are carefully recorded and broken into the following units: *Episodes of consciousness* are continuous periods of consciousness separated by holes in the flow of consciousness."

This is similar to what I find when interviewing a student on his or her meditation sitting. There are periods of meditative experience that are continuous and remembered as distinct events or sequences (having continuity), as well as gaps in the experience, where either the person has no memory or is certain that nothing happened. These are most definitely felt as holes in the flow of consciousness, of which, in meditation, there are many types. No matter how mindful someone is in meditation, there will be gaps, there will be experiences that will go on under the radar, and there will be limited recall of the meditation sitting. Only by going into a detailed recollection of your experiences will you discover that this movement from continuity to discontinuity and back to continuity again is how our consciousness works, and this is how awareness, at its most basic level, functions. Awareness relies on some kind of continuity of experience and is usually not trained to take in anything discontinuous. But through Recollective Awareness, it can go into those areas of experience that seemed outside of ordinary awareness because of their haziness, lack of definition, meaninglessness, confusing qualities, blankness, and the like. I am not talking about a higher-level constant awareness of a bright and alert equanimous observer but about cultivating awareness of what we are usually not aware of as a means to becoming more aware.

Both mindfulness and Recollective Awareness are ways of becoming aware of what you have been aware of. Mindfulness is awareness in the present moment of what you are presently aware of. Recollective Awareness is awareness in the present moment of what you were aware of at some point in the past. Both of these forms of awareness-meditation practice have their advantages and disadvantages. But I don't want to debate the pros and cons of these two practices; I just want to clarify that they use different theories of awareness to inform their respective meditation practices.

Recollective Awareness uses your memory to bring about greater awareness of the full range of your inner experience, while mindfulness uses a directed attention on specific parts of your experience in the present moment. By using your memory of experiences that have happened, you become more familiar with them and thus find yourself more conscious and aware of them when they happen again. This produces an awareness of what is going on in the present moment about which the meditator is not self-consciously trying to be aware. You just start to notice how a familiar feeling comes over you, and the thoughts and intentions you have with it, and you become aware of how you are being with it—there is no directive to now focus on that feeling or bring it more into awareness or to become mindful of it in such a way that it vanishes. This is because you have been practicing awareness of emotions by first allowing them to form and develop as they will and then recollecting them afterward rather than trying to catch them when they arise and bring your attention to them in the body. An active, directed awareness, as in much of mindfulness practice, operates on the notion that awareness in the present moment is the only valid form of awareness, for it catches experiences when they arise and knows them directly. Awareness of one part of the experience, say the breath or a bodily sensation, is sufficient for one to be mindful of it in the present. What may be important here for a Vipassana practitioner of mindfulness is knowing the arising and passing away of that part of experience, while for someone practicing Recollective Awareness meditation, the knowledge of the various aspects of the experience that keep it going is of greater importance than simply knowing that it arose and passed away. For that reason, Recollective Awareness meditation is generally more suited to those Vipassana meditators who are seeking to understand the nature of causality (or conditionality) within their experience.

The basic level of awareness in the theory of Recollective Awareness is the type (or degree) of awareness found in the various states of consciousness a person experiences. The next level of awareness is found in the recollection of the state of mind one experienced. This second-level awareness is actually similar to what is developed in mindfulness meditation practice, except in Recollective Awareness meditation practice it is less focused on a particular part of one's experience and more inclusive of the whole experience. Since it is done after the fact, it is detached from the experience in time, while in mindfulness practice the detachment may be seen more as occurring in space (both the knowing and the experience known are meant to occur in the present moment). Though this kind of awareness of knowing an experience can happen in Recollective Awareness meditation practice, because of the theory of awareness that's being employed, there is no notion of a simultaneous witness to an experience and the experience itself; rather, you know that the in breath you were aware of happened before you were aware of your awareness of it. What is inserted here, in terms of a theory, is a reflective awareness that makes our more basic sense experience explicit to us after it has first arisen. This reflective awareness happens so fast that it is impossible to stop. It puts language to an experience, it gives a sense of a self who experiences it, and thus it makes the experience known to us as having a certain form, tone, texture, name. This reflective awareness gives us the capacity to step outside of the physical experience or the emotional reaction or the thought impulse and look back at it. Once there is a moment of reflective awareness of a sense-door experience, we can't go back to its just being a sense-door experience—that kind of awareness moves our experience into another realm, and from then on that sense experience, be it a sound, sight, smell, sensation, or idea, is bound up in a process of naming, thinking about, manipulating, navigating, and so on. It can never go back to being just a pure sense experience, which it never was in the first place, because once it was known reflectively, that is, consciously with awareness, it began a life in the mind, from which it can never escape. All one can have is an idea of what the pure sense experience might have been like, but in truth, that would be an imagination about a pure sense experience.

This process reminds me of the Buddha's teaching on *papañca,* which often gets translated as "proliferation," though it is a Pali word for a particular kind of deluded thinking. Unfortunately, when people read the Madhupindika Sutta (the Honey Ball Sutta), where the snowball effect of *papañca* is described, they think in terms of a linear process that leads to the proliferation of deluded ideas instead of a loop of deluded ideas informing how we, as human beings, process sense and thought impressions.

Our reflective awareness, whether it is mindfulness or Recollective Awareness, tampers with our experiences, distorts them, and creates kinds of untruth in our mind. That is the consequence of our awareness of what we are aware of. It gives us things we think we know. People steeped in meditation literature and practice may say, "Whoa, let's stop the train here and get off." They may have the belief that all we need to do is still our minds and go beyond thoughts and emotions, and all of this unreality will dissolve in a realization of the truth. And that is a path some people do choose to take. But it is not a path of developing greater awareness. If you want to become an aware human being, you can't stop there.

Actually, this is where we are prompted to develop a third level of awareness. I prefer to conceptualize this type of awareness as an outgrowth of reflective awareness, an enhancement of it, a knowing of how one's mind knows things that can correct certain errors that are created through an unbridled reflective awareness. It is not some kind of pure awareness but, rather, a purifying type of awareness. It doesn't just know how you know something, like following an infinite recession of images in facing mirrors; instead, it opens up to a whole new perspective on the experiences that were known reflectively. It is not linear. There can be many moments, hours, days, and even years between the experience known reflectively in error and then later corrected.

We have all seen movies or read stories where a character wakes up out of a deluded fog and realizes that what he believed before is now false. Most everyone has experienced this at least once in his or her life. For some people this kind of insight is a realization, a waking up to something profound that was possible to be known all along but wasn't. And when one wakes up like this, one can't really go back to sleep. That is one aspect of this kind of awareness: it wakes you up about something. It opens your eyes to a certain questionable habit or behavior, and if you don't stop doing it, at least you can't go back to doing it in ignorance. Because of awareness of the moral or ethical problems, you can no longer turn a blind eye. But your ordinary second-level reflective awareness can. It can just label the dilemma as not a problem or create a story that justifies some kind of harmful action or assert a rule or principle that makes the action acceptable. Such awareness can be trained to notice harmful intentions with indifference or detachment, but once you become aware of the delusion of seeing a harmful intention with indifference, you can't be indifferent to it without awareness of it, and its consequences, anymore.

There is nothing to be gained by mystifying this third level of awareness or saying that it is out of reach for most people or can be arrived at only through certain meditation practices and not others. I do not doubt that people who practice mindfulness meditation also develop their awareness of knowing how they have known their experience. This level of awareness is also to be found in people who practice Eugene Gendlin's Focusing, Stern's microanalytic interview, or any number of sound psychological practices for increasing one's awareness of sensations, emotions, perceptions, ideas, intentions, and narratives. It may be something that certain individuals quite naturally develop in their lives without doing any particular practice whatsoever.

What is it that really differentiates this third-level awareness from a second-level awareness? It is essentially found in the awareness of subjective experience. For instance, there are many meditators I know who are able to hear the differences in birdsongs and are readily able to identify which bird they heard. They are reflectively aware of the sound each bird makes, since they recognize it and can name it. When they hear a bird chirp or warble or screech, they may also feel something, such as joy, irritation, or a pleasant memory. If they begin recalling their subjective responses to the birdsongs, rather than just identifying the bird by its call, their awareness moves away from identifying sounds to being with emotions, memories, thoughts. The distinction I am making here can easily be seen as the difference between a bird-watcher out to note the birds she sees and hears and a poet or artist who is trying to express seeing, hearing, experiencing birds.

This is why we may turn to artists, poets, and writers to help us understand our inner world. For them, expressing how they know their experience, along with a keen awareness or memory of those experiences, is what they do. They have practice doing this. And so do many people who meditate in ways that promote and develop awareness further than it has gone before.

Can meditation practices that teach students to go beyond their thoughts and emotions and enter into states of mind that are still, peaceful, and uncluttered lead to this level of awareness? I don't think there is a clear answer to that. If such awareness does arise, how does it happen, since it is not part of the practice one is doing? To me, this is mysterious. It is one reason I have been mostly skeptical of meditation practices that claim to lead to an instant enlightenment or awakening. Meditation practices that are pragmatic, such as mindfulness and Recollective Awareness, have the development of awareness as an integral part of the practice. You can see it grow and evolve in students over time. There is no mystery to it. It is like learning a foreign language—the new learning grows upon existing skills and learning and does not happen all of a sudden.

I would like to continue this exploration of awareness using an excerpt from a meditator's journal. He is a former Buddhist monk who returned to the lay life several years ago. The passage reads: *Notice tension in my back, some body twitching, feeling like I have not got anywhere with my life, noticing that the conflict I feel around my views of letting go has not allowed me to think through my life and the choices I could make, feeling overwhelmed by my different tasks, noticing that the overwhelm is mainly me not allowing thoughts about what I need to do arise, the view that it is more important for me to sit than do the practical things that need doing.*

In terms of use of language when describing experiences, his use of the word *feeling* seems to indicate a second-level awareness of the experience, while the word *noticing* is used for a third-level awareness of the experience. There are two instances of this:

1. *Feeling* like he has not gotten anywhere with his life and *noticing* the conflict between his views of letting go (abandoning, surrendering, giving up) and thinking through choices (holding on to thoughts, examining them, making an informed choice)
2. *Feeling* overwhelmed by his different tasks and *noticing* that the overwhelm has to do with not allowing thoughts about what he needs to do

Starting with the first example, he is aware that he is thinking about not having gotten anywhere in life and, I assume that when he feels that way, he believes it is a fact. The feeling of not having gotten anywhere with his life is a story about his life, one that he believes in. So he can know that he feels that way, but where does that actually get him? In the past, he may have just tried to let go of those thoughts and move on. The intention to do just that does arise for him, for how else could he just then feel the conflict between the letting go and the taking up of those thoughts? He can't simply take up the thoughts and feelings about his life, since he has repeatedly discounted them in meditation, so what he experiences is the conflict. He then turns his attention to the conflict of how he handled the thoughts about his life not getting anywhere rather than to trying to think through how to get somewhere in his life. His awareness of feeling that he is not getting anywhere in life is the basis for him to now become aware of how he has been knowing those thoughts and feelings in meditation.

As you can see, the third-level awareness is not just a straight line of becoming aware of his thoughts and feelings but, rather, an expansion of awareness to include what it is that has made it difficult for him to become fully aware of how he has been relating to and handling those thoughts and feelings. This is a natural progression, since you may need to become aware of what has been obscuring your awareness and understanding before you can develop a more refined and accurate awareness and understanding of yourself. And in this case, the idea is not to try to get through the conflict or tension that you discover but to notice it more clearly as coming into being when you have certain thoughts and feelings. Otherwise, you probably get stuck in loops of second-level self-reflective awareness, which has the flavor of trying to correct the situation prematurely, of letting go of it, or of succumbing to the perceived futility of it. You may have to go through a period of being stuck in these loops until you can notice the conflict and tension in ways that enable you to know it more clearly, to penetrate it with your intelligent interest and compassion.

The second example from this person's meditation sitting exemplifies an even greater challenge to the development of awareness. When feeling overwhelmed by thoughts and feelings, the impulse is to have them stop, not to allow them to go on. The different tasks that he is thinking about seem overwhelming to him. But as he notices his thoughts, he is able to look at the experience of being overwhelmed rather than the tasks he is thinking about. This shift of attention takes him out of thinking about doing the tasks and brings him to why he has not allowed himself to think about these tasks in meditation. He is then able to get at the view that has been operating beneath (or alongside) the conflict he experienced earlier between letting go of thoughts and holding on to them for a while longer. This view is not clearly articulated in his journal entry, but I believe it is something akin to "spirituality is superior to materiality." That is, it is more important to devote time and energy to one's spiritual progress than it is to put more effort into one's worldly success. As a monk for many years, he no doubt labored under the notion that the spiritual life was superior to the worldly life and that the worldly life just took care of itself and didn't require any serious attention, while the spiritual life required constant effort. If he never became aware of this view and how it was affecting his choices in meditation and in his life, then he would be entirely subject to it. Here, in this particular sitting, he is able to notice it coming up at a time when he is in conflict about whether to think about practical matters (the different tasks) or let go of those thoughts and thereby bypass them again.

One of the main ways that a third-level awareness stops the repetitive loops of self-reflective awareness is in the noticing of underlying views and beliefs that have supported notions on how to bypass or correct certain inner conflicts. Once the views are known and examined, the bypassing and correcting can actually begin to fall away. What is left is the meditator facing himself honestly in his meditation, trusting that his mind will be able to expand his awareness to take in what is truly feeding and supporting the impasse he is in. This is not a quick and easy process—but once you begin to notice it and understand how it works, it is never too far away.

10

Exploring Transformative
Conceptualization

What do I mean by transformative conceptualization?

The most common metaphor for transformation is that of metamorphosis: a caterpillar morphing into a chrysalis and from there turning into a butterfly. This template of metamorphosis gets applied to spiritual practices and creates a good deal of confusion. Humans do not become anything other than human beings through spiritual practice. What the various religious traditions tend to teach, however, is that they become something special or divine after they die. But we can't prove that kind of transformation and so have to take it on faith or just not believe it. Perhaps the metamorphosis metaphor has run its course and we need to replace it with something a bit more down-to-earth and practical.

So I'll propose a metaphor closer to our modern sensibility. I remember, when I took Chemistry 101, the teacher saying that a chemical change is like making toast. You start with a fresh, soft slice of bread, put it in the toaster, and out comes a browned, hard, crunchy piece of toast. There is a causal relation between the slice of bread and the piece of toast, but they are not the same thing, because by your heating the bread for a few minutes, it is no longer bread but toast. Of course, the human mind is much more complex and varied than bread, but we tend to do something similar with our spiritual and psychological "progress" and think of it as a form of transformation. We change in ways that are consistent with our temperament or psyche and do not become a different person but are noticeably different from the way we were before. We are not the same person: we can't actually go backward, just like you can't change toast into bread, though we may still have many of the same habits of mind and hold on to things that preceded the change; perhaps, then, our only error is the assumption that something else changed in the transformation that really didn't change. Then there is no going backward, there is just the rearising of something that hasn't changed that we mistakenly thought had. This happens frequently in spiritual practice.

Conceptualization is often looked at negatively in spiritual practices, particularly Buddhist-influenced ones, as it takes one away from the direct experience. Many spiritual seekers are looking for experiences of oneness, emptiness, truth, transcendent reality, and so forth, and are not interested in concepts about these things. Why should they be? Such heightened spiritual accomplishments exist beyond concepts. They are known without relying on any conceptualizing process; that is how these things are often taught.

But there are several problems with this point of view. Spiritual experiences end. People come out of them, or even if they last a long time, someday the person comes down from them. This leaves a memory of the experience (or the realization). Such memories form the basis for an after story. It is the after story that the person carries around with him. It is the story of oneness, emptiness, truth, enlightenment, that is told to others. The experience is not communicated without the use of concepts, unless he has some magical way of having another person experience what he has experienced.

A transformative conceptualization is an after story of an experience of transformation. Such stories may be what sustain the changes in thought and behavior that were planted by the initial experience or realization. They are what make the experience or realization credible to others. These are the stories that raise people up into the status of spiritual masters and adepts and can be used as some kind of currency to win over followers. This is why so many spiritual leaders have not had to live up to their teachings—a transformative conceptualization has kept their attainments and realizations alive. The experience of enlightenment or purity that the conceptualization is based on is long in the past, capable only of acting on the level of concepts, stories, narratives, beliefs.

You might want to argue with me that experiences and realizations truly change people in deeper and more meaningful ways than keeping a story alive about a past attainment. I won't deny the transformative power of certain meditative states and realizations—they really can have a lasting effect on the texture, feel, and activity of one's mind. You can feel softer, friendlier, more understanding and compassionate, mysteriously wiser than you could ever have imagined from such experiences, but that is just how you have changed. When you articulate that change to yourself and then to others, according to characteristics of an enlightened person in a particular tradition, then it turns into a story.

When a transformative conceptualization goes in the right direction, it follows a simple schema that I laid out in my previous book, *Unlearning Meditation*. First you are aware of the existing conceptualization, which has usually become rigid and fixed by this time and often takes on a particular label or identity. Then comes questioning, doubting the validity or credibility of that fixed label. The process can then open up to looking at the experiences without using the label. This will lead to new awareness and discernment of those types of experiences (memories, thoughts, emotions, and the like) and to fresh descriptions of them. Those new descriptions will produce a new narrative, one that is a bit more accurate and more fluid, and is capable of bringing about further investigation instead of stopping investigation altogether (as the fixed label often does). Through this process, the initial conceptualization, the one with a fixed label, can be abandoned, or its influence may be diminished. Transformative conceptualization is a process of abandoning or diminishing the influence of faulty views and narratives and arriving at views and narratives that come about through examination. You could liken it to the scientific method, except instead of having the goal of arriving at a truth about the physical world (arrived at through experimentation and verification), the result here is knowledge and wisdom of your inner world, where there is no absolute truth.

Questioning an attainment, whether it be self-assessed or granted by a teacher, is not an easy thing to do. I pray that you will never be told you have an attainment, and if you have been, that you are willing to doubt its validity. But what I would say about questioning attainments is also applicable to any fixed identity or label you have been given or have given yourself. It is just that an attainment is a positive label, and as such, there is less incentive to doubt it. Who would willingly question their accomplishments, their greatness, their specialness, since these conceits have historically given people pleasure and power?

It is true that I am skeptical of all attainments. I believe attainments are unnecessary concepts. They can easily derail a well-functioning spiritual path and turn it into a dysfunctional nightmare. In spiritual communities, those individuals who are seen as having attainments can be idealized by others and have enormous power over them. It is easy for psychopaths and narcissists to claim attainments, for they may already believe in their innate superiority to everyone else and use that identity for their own selfish or cruel ends. And oddly enough, the unemotional and self-controlled persona of a psychopath can easily deceive gullible people into believing him to be spiritually advanced, especially if the tradition values steely detachment and superficial self-control.

Some attainments may be real. Now, when that is the case, there is no advantage to making it known. Someone who really has succeeded in diminishing the force of her desires and ill will, and has substantially reduced her self-importance and pride, would be content being a nobody. The worldly pursuits of success, fame, and wealth would not matter to her. Having power over others would be meaningless and more a burden than a dream fulfilled. I can see no reason why someone who has actually attained a degree of awakening (or liberation) would want to make it known to people, who would then make something out of her that would make her life more unpleasant and complicated.

Seeking Nibbana

In my novel *Seeking Nibbana in Sri Lanka,* one of the main characters, a Sri Lankan meditation master by the name of Venerable Aggachitta, goes through a process of questioning the attainment of *sotapanna* ("stream-entry," the first path and fruit) that his Burmese teacher bestowed upon him more than two decades earlier. When the novel opens, Aggachitta is perceived by people who have heard of him as an arhat living in the forest. He, however, is sure that he is not an arhat, but he does not know whether he is still a *sotapanna* or if he has advanced further and is now a *sakadagami* (the second path and fruit) or, further yet, an *anagami* (the third path and fruit).

He does not start by doubting that he is a *sotapanna,* as that would be too painful, too destabilizing. Whenever his investigation gets close to doubting his attainment, he quickly diverts his attention elsewhere. Instead, he digs around the attainment without touching it, for that is psychologically safer. Remember, he has believed he is a *sotapanna* for more than two decades; he became a monk on account of it and left the world to live in the forest in order to take this attainment further. So he begins by examining the criteria by which he was evaluated to be a *sotapanna.* This includes the beliefs and views he holds on meditation practice, on the Buddha's teaching, and on *nibbana.*

Having been a Buddhist scholar before he decided to become a monk, Aggachitta has his own thesis on the Buddha's teaching of Dependent Arising, which he wrote about in his dissertation more than twenty years earlier and would like to modify to include his current thinking. His thesis is summed up on page 17:

His mind goes to the memory of his dissertation on conditionality and his intellect adroitly latches on to the conundrum of Buddhist causality. Simply put, in order for there to be no self, the basic principle of the Buddha's original teaching on conditionality has to be violated. This principle, which states that "when one thing arises, so does another," describing a link between two things, a connection that cannot be severed, is violated by the theory of momentariness, which states, "when one state of consciousness vanishes, another state immediately arises." In his thesis, Aggachitta proves that the doctrine of momentariness is essential in preserving the doctrine of no-self from being corrupted with views of self. Then he goes on to state that the original formulation of conditionality was in no uncertain terms only meant to cover the cycle of renewed existence and not operations in the mental present moment.

As you can see, he is quite an intellectual, but don't let that deter you. He is following the Buddhist commentarial tradition in this interpretation of Dependent Arising. There is no new thinking involved here. The theory of consciousness is one where consciousness arises and passes away millions of times a second, though it gives the appearance of being one continuous thing. Following the logic of this theory, there can be no such thing as a self because the truth of consciousness is that it is constantly arising and vanishing and can never be found in a stable state. Dependent Arising, on the other hand, refers to an interdependent relationship between things, and if that view is applied to our experience of consciousness, then it is possible for views of self to creep in because now there is duration to experience, which is the basis for the notion of an enduring self. So Aggachitta sees it as necessary to treat Dependent Arising as pertaining to how the previous life created the karma for this life and how this life creates the karma for the next one. It has nothing to do with how consciousness functions in the moment, supposedly.

Then one day an old friend, Venerable Maggaphala, pays

Aggachitta a surprise visit at his forest hermitage. He brings Aggachitta a copy of an article on Dependent Arising written by an American scholar who takes a different slant on it. This writer proposes that Dependent Arising describes the basic inherent structures of our mental experience. It is not about the previous life, this life, and the one following. As a Westerner, he might not even believe in rebirth. Rather, he sees it as something more practical: "Dependent arising (*paticca-samuppada*) has traditionally been interpreted as a sequence of events that arise in linear fashion over a given period of time. This has led people to believe that the links in the chain of dependent arising can be separated and thus viewed as isolated elements. When the Buddha proclaimed, 'When this is, that is so,' did he mean, 'From this being so, that arose' or did he mean, 'This being so, that is'? I am of the opinion that he meant 'This being so, that is.'"

Aggachitta is immediately critical of this position. It disturbs him that an obviously educated and intelligent person can think this way. For what really bothers him is that this author has disagreed with Aggachitta's prized thesis, merely by asserting that he believes the Buddha meant that two or more things (consciousness, name and form, perception, feeling, intention, desire, and so on) arise together ("this being so, that is") rather than the more doctrinaire position of one thing arising after another ("from this being so, that arose"). This simple disagreement spurs Aggachitta to leave the forest hermitage briefly and stay at a monastery with a library in order to do the necessary research to find out where he stands on the teaching of Dependent Arising.

Now, why is this pursuit so important? Namely, because the Buddha taught that he who sees Dependent Arising sees the Dhamma. Someone who sees the Dhamma is at least a *sotapanna*. So all *sotapanna*s must correctly understand Dependent Arising. If one of them doesn't, maybe he isn't a *sotapanna* after all.

Before I go on with Aggachitta's story, I will need to digress for a few paragraphs.

A person's identity is here being indirectly questioned. This can be a disturbing process in itself, but it often feels safer and more secure than questioning the identification directly. So let's bring this into a more familiar arena by looking at a person's identification as a good meditator because he has few or no thoughts in meditation and can usually get into calm, peaceful states that last for much of the sitting. The idea in investigating his meditative experience is not to attack the notion that he is a good meditator. For if I did that during an interview, he probably would not trust me. His story about being a good meditator, and what he presents that supports it, is enough for me to accept that his meditation practice has mostly gone well. I am happy for him. But I would like for him to become more accepting of his thoughts and emotions and to develop greater awareness of them, and for that to happen, he will need to get a sense of what it is like to meditate with thoughts and emotions. In doing so, he may perceive himself as a bad meditator. But that story is not true either. He will then develop other narratives of himself as a meditator as his practice continues that will be based on his honest awareness of what goes on when he meditates. The prior values of a good meditator, who is predominantly free of thoughts while meditating, will have been questioned with the incorporation of other values, such as becoming patient and wise with his thoughts. Along with that, the notion of a good meditator will become fuzzy, unclear, and eventually unnecessary. He is simply an honest meditator.

"An honest meditator" is how I see the concept of *sappurisa* as found in the Buddha's discourses. *Sappurisa* is often translated as "a true man" or "a good person," and Venerable Thanissaro translates it as "a person of integrity." To my knowledge, this concept does not fit into any theory of stages on the path to full awakening. Rather, it seems to be a way of discussing the qualities of someone who is on the Buddha's path to full awakening and someone who isn't. It is clear that an individual does not possess these qualities on account of birth or upbringing, fame or status, gain or privilege, or through the practice of certain rites and rituals. He "puts the practice of the way" to liberation first and does not make more out of himself or disparage others in the process. According to *The Shorter Discourse on the Full-Moon Night,* the qualities of a true man or honest meditator (or person of integrity) are faith, shame, fear of wrongdoing, learning, energy, mindfulness, and wisdom.

There is another interesting feature of an honest meditator, and I would like to quote a passage from Bhikkhu Bodhi's translation of "The True Man" in *The Middle Length Discourses of the Buddha*.

"But the true man considers thus: 'Non-identification even with the attainment of the first jhana has been declared by the Blessed One; for in whatever way they conceive, the fact is ever other than that.' So, putting non-identification first, he neither lauds himself nor disparages others because of his attainment of the first jhana. This too is the character of a true man."

So here we have an honest meditator who does not identify with the higher states of consciousness at which he has arrived in his practice. He builds no conceit about himself having experienced it, neither holding himself above others on account of it nor disparaging those who may not have experienced this kind of higher consciousness. And there is something here for those who do not identify with such states of consciousness: they are open to explore those experiences as they arise for them again, knowing that "whatever way they conceive, the fact is ever other than that." That is, in my interpretation of what is said here, the conceptualization of inner states of mind can only be but an approximate representation of those states and that there is ever more to learn about them. But you can't learn anything more about them if the concepts remain fixed and rigid.

Now we can go back to the fictional Venerable Aggachitta's search for *nibbana*. He continues without the need to identify experiences and understandings as belonging to a particular stage. He is seeking to understand the nature of Dependent Arising and from that to more clearly understand *nibbana,* rather than seeking to arrive at the next stage on the path to full awakening. He questions the map that was used by his teacher to determine his attainment of the first stage after he realizes that he cannot adequately use it to plot his new meditation student's progress. And this same map would be used to determine the attainment of the next three stages for himself. So he puts it aside. He thus tries to seek *nibbana* without having his concepts about it interfere with his progress. But he can't really do it because he knows too much Buddhist philosophy and too many stories, metaphors, and formulas, and he has already thought through too many arguments of Buddhist views he agrees with and those he's against. His mind is too set in its way to do this kind of search in an open, inquisitive manner, and yet he is incredibly well equipped to do it, because he knows what is not *nibbana,* at least conceptually. That is, if he gets fooled by a false experience or understanding of *nibbana,* he will be able to see through that deception and right his course. This is really what transformative conceptualization is about: correcting errors in our way of seeing, not adding more errors to the mix.

This type of error-correcting seeing is a dynamic process that does not end with "the true story" but, rather, examines the various stories that come up when you seek greater understanding (enlightenment, awakening, liberation, whatever you prefer to call it). In many respects, it partakes of a healthy skeptical attitude, where you remain skeptical of your concepts about things that you have not experienced yet. Instead of trying to get your experiences to match ideas of what they should be, which unfortunately has infiltrated a good many spiritual practices, you attend closely to your experiences, and from that awareness and discernment, you modify your ideas accordingly. Without certain ideas, however, you might miss things about your experience, so the direction here is not some unrealistic abandoning of all preconceived notions but the use of concepts that have come to you from people wiser and more experienced in this area than you. For the fictional Venerable Aggachitta, the Buddha is one such wise person who has gone the path he wishes to trod, so he takes what the Buddha says as a reliable guide.

The Buddha's teachings on *nibbana* come with centuries of commentary, opinion, folklore, superstition, and arguments, so it is not easy for someone to sort through all of that and find something reliable. From all that he has read, studied, and heard, Aggachitta has to get to what he believes are trustworthy and personally verifiable teachings.

In his search for *nibbana*, he first takes it on faith that *nibbana* is not a mental state one experiences. This brings him close to the view that *nibbana* is some kind of transcendent reality that exists outside ordinary reality and is the basis for the wholesome, true, correct functioning of reality. This view tends to call *nibbana* the unconditioned, while the ordinary world people inhabit is conditioned. The unconditioned is therefore stable, permanent, detached. It is too easy for one to fall into a belief of an eternal higher self with this view, so someone who has seen and understands Dependent Arising would have to put aside the notion of the permanence and stability of anything. This person would have to hold two contradictory views: (1) that things are in flux and dependent on conditions and (2) that something exists that is stable and unconditioned. Many wise people before Venerable Aggachitta have held these contradictory views without much inner conflict, but for him, one of these has to be put aside in his search for *nibbana*. He can't be looking at the impermanent, changing, and conditioned nature of his experience while at the same time holding some idea that there is something permanent, unchanging, and unconditioned underneath (or beyond) it all. So he jettisons the concept of *nibbana*'s being unconditioned and eternal, which he believes the Buddha would have done in his situation, and treats the concept of *nibbana*'s being unconditioned skeptically as a possibility to be confirmed when he arrives at a complete and verifiable understanding of *nibbana*. But for now, the unconditioned is just a concept that hinders his investigation into the truth of his experience.

In this way he moves in the direction of the view that there is no such thing as *nibbana* (as some absolute transcendent reality). If there is *nibbana,* it has to be found in the conditioned world of his senses, thoughts, and emotions. In that case, *nibbana* must be the no-self found in his everyday life. It is his experience of eating, walking, talking, and doing things without a sense of self. He even reframes it as "*nibbana* eats for the arhat." That is, there is no being that is an arhat that eats food; for an arhat, it is *nibbana* (no-self) that eats. And for a while, he can be drawn into that view and find it valid. Then, as he wakes up to the implications of this new view, he becomes skeptical about it. It doesn't end his search for *nibbana;* in fact, it takes him off course, for anybody can experience eating, walking, doing things as no-self, at least for short periods of time. It doesn't mean you have understood *nibbana* or purified your mind or severed the fetters that bind you to renewed existence (including the repetition of certain harmful thoughts and emotions).

The transformative conceptualization that will guide him further on his search for *nibbana* is reached in the final paragraphs of the novel, which I reproduce here:

> Aggachitta goes to his desk and picks up the exercise book where he has been jotting down his recent thoughts. He flips through it to see if he may have written something in the last few days on this new approach to meditation, but all he finds are his philosophical musings. The musings are what his mind does to articulate certain kinds of understandings, but they do not speak of a practice, or of a path. He wrote at length about the path, though he never described how meditation fits in with it. To correct this omission, he intends to write something about it. He picks up his notebook and flips it open to the page where he wrote:
>
> "It is not a gap, not a loss of consciousness, but a clear space of knowing the act of knowing."
>
> When he wrote that sentence he was conceiving of a pure consciousness that knows the process of knowing. From his current perspective, he was describing an ideal state of consciousness, one that he would now attribute a temporary existence to, rather than as something eternal and absolute. He now wonders if indeed such an ideal, pure consciousness can exist at all, and if it is just a habit of mind for him to conceive of such a consciousness. What would his experience of "a clear space of knowing the act of knowing" be if knowing the act of knowing was just a mentally fabricated concept? If that were the case, then the

knowing he had considered to be pure would have perception and experience in it, and so it would not be nirodha, where perception and experience ceases, leaving only consciousness. Just as there is no separation of knowing from the known, there can be no higher knowing that exists without perception and experience.

Then his mind flashes to nirodha thus being impossible. Then, because of that, nibbana does not exist. And then, as a crescendo, a realization that all concepts have no reality other than their mental existence, and therefore all he knows about nibbana and the path is not real, a figment, a mirage. After a second of utter despair at there being nothing salvageable from these realizations, a marvelous and sublime understanding occurs to him:

Samsara is such.

Nibbana is the final knowing of that.

Why this has not occurred to him before is the first thought that occurs to him now. The answer is clear. His view of consciousness, despite all he had believed about its emptiness, impermanence, no-self, and suffering, was still conceptual. As much as he would like to contemplate this further, he knows that whatever it was he understood is now past, and beyond retrieval.

By this very description, I could say that his realization was non-conceptual. The realization itself, and those like it, may have no words or story arising with them. But after it happens, it takes on some form of conceptualization. What Aggachitta realizes after this realization is that it is beyond retrieval. All that can now come from it are concepts about it, ways of bringing it into one's life, and ways of communicating it to others. The novel ends here, with him doing nothing about his realization. But in practice, that is often not the case.

The Buddha's own story was one of deciding whether to teach or not after his night of awakening. In order to teach, he had to conceptualize his understanding so that he could communicate his path to liberation. The first thing he conceptualized was the teaching on Dependent Arising. After that, it was the teaching on the ceasing of Dependent Arising. And from that it was a simple step to the Four Noble Truths and the Noble Eightfold Path. What we have twenty-six hundred years later is not his realization but his teaching after his awakening.

So when some people versed in the Buddha's teaching hear my theory of transformative conceptualization, they reply with the simile of the raft, which, in brief, says: In order to get to an island, you will need a raft, and once you have reached the island, carrying the raft around with you is absurd. That is, once you have a nonconceptual understanding, it is no longer necessary to carry around those concepts.

I read this simile a bit differently, as you might expect. The Buddha talks about building a very good raft, not a shoddy one. It is a reference to the well-built raft of his teaching. Though it may not be of use when someone experiences a nonconceptual understanding, it probably was of great use in helping him get there, and the improved raft may be of use to others who wish to make the same crossing.

Provisional Truths

I could easily have ended my explanation of transformative conceptualization here but for one last important point. This process does not seem to end. As much as anyone would like to be done once and for all with questioning, searching, doubting, and examining one's experiences and understandings in meditation, the final story never seems completely final, at least for me. Instead of the final truth, the last word, what I keep finding are provisional truths that are more honest and accurate understandings than those I held before and generally function as new improved narratives (concepts) that form the basis for the next round of investigation into the nature of meditative (and psychological) experience.

In this way of looking at things, a great transformative realization is not final; it is a stepping stone for other realizations. Without this transformative realization, you may not be able to go past some limits in your meditation practice. But when it is turned into a final realization, that creates a new limit. When it becomes provisional, it can lead to opening up to new experiences and insights. So it might seem that you should stop at the great realization and not go any further—only you can't really stop because your mind, and your life, won't stop.

Accepting the nature of change in our lives makes provisional truths, rather than unchanging truths, a necessity. It reduces the attachment to views, opinions, and beliefs. It makes it so there is less fighting, arguing, defending, and upholding of causes and ideals. Such acceptance of the changing provisional nature of our ideas of what is true about ourselves and others humbles us and makes us reconsider each time we get some new information.

As human beings, we are never finished works. In a spiritual practice that accepts our mind/body experience as being dependent on causes and conditions, there is no final stopping place. There are just periods of relief from suffering and not building upon what creates suffering. And if it makes me less of a Buddhist to say I don't believe in an end point, it may also make me more of a Buddhist to say, with compassion, it is all right to be with what you experience, to stay with it, to know it, to look into it, and to let go of it. Thoughts do not have to end for inner peace to arise. Thoughts, really, are not the enemy.

11

Maturation of the Meditative Process

A mature meditation practice is a reliable one. It is a refuge, a place to go when you need to look at something about yourself, to process a difficult emotion or situation (or decision), to question a belief or a teaching, to connect with your inner world, or to consider new directions in your life and in your relationships.

At first your meditation practice, no matter what practice you start with, is immature. In its immaturity it may be a struggle to do at times, seem unclear and be filled with doubts, and yet produce some new and powerful experiences and insights. It needs to be fed and nurtured from the outside as well as within, but may require additional dependence on a teacher, tradition, or belief system. It can't quite stand on its own two feet.

I am reminded of the story of the Buddha's first attendant monk, Meghiya. One day, while going out for alms, Meghiya saw a lovely mango grove. The beauty and serenity of the grove so caught his attention that he decided this was the place for him to meditate in his pursuit of *nibbana*. He asked the Buddha to give him leave to meditate in this wonderful mango grove, and the Buddha denied his first request. He asked again, and the Buddha denied his second request. With the third request, the Buddha relented and let him go.

Meghiya meditated in this mango grove and found his mind being drawn toward unwholesome thoughts, thoughts that were not worthy of a *bhikkhu,* namely thoughts of lust and violence. He couldn't get through these thoughts, he couldn't see how they were fueled, and they refused to subside after some days meditating. So he left the mango grove and returned to the Buddha. What the Buddha said at this time to Meghiya is well worth noting:

"When one's practice is immature, Meghiya, there are five things that are conducive to liberation of mind that should be matured. What are these five?

"Here, for an immature practice, the first thing that is conducive to liberation of mind that should be matured in one's practice is a Good Friend, who is enduring and knows you well."

Meditation practice, especially these days, is not about going off to the forest and meditating in total isolation but is something that is done while living in the world. Meditating in itself is an isolating activity, so why make it more so by separating yourself from other human beings? Your meditation practice can be supported by a community of like-minded meditators and teachers whose main role is to aid you in your development in meditation and not rope you into some kind of cult or take advantage of you for their own ends.

Some people who have read my books and articles have gotten the erroneous message that I am teaching a type of do-it-yourself meditation, where you don't need a teacher and can progress just fine completely on your own. If that were indeed the case, I wouldn't have invested so much time and energy over the past dozen years in training teachers and further refining how this approach to meditation is taught. Although I have seen people at workshops and retreats who have read my writings or listened to my talks and have told me that they are practicing Recollective Awareness meditation, practically all of them say that they finally get what I am talking about after having meditated with me—that there was something they just couldn't get their head around in the book, and now they can see more clearly what this practice is about.

That is part of the reason for my writing this book. After *Unlearning Meditation* came out, many people who read the book apparently didn't realize that this approach allows thinking to go on in meditation. They read it, but it seemed to have gotten buried in that book, so I wrote this book to excavate that core element of this meditation practice and put it on display. No doubt there are aspects of Recollective Awareness meditation that are only briefly touched upon in this book and will have to be brought out in future books. And you can always decide to work with a Recollective Awareness meditation teacher and learn this approach in the way meditation has been taught for centuries—from a living person who gives you teachings, listens to your experiences, and offers guidance and wisdom.

A Recollective Awareness Meditation Teacher

I taught this approach to meditation for twelve years before training another teacher in it. At first I didn't think it was possible to train someone to teach in this way, not because it required some special ability, but because I had to figure out what was at the heart of teaching this type of meditation practice and how to teach just that. So what is at the heart of Recollective Awareness meditation?

Your own experience of meditation. It is the honest and open recounting of what goes on in your meditation sittings. A teacher would therefore have to learn how to listen to a wide range of meditation experiences, and not with an ear as to the correct or right experiences but, rather, a willingness to hear and an interest in hearing, all that is going on in a meditator's sittings.

When I train teachers, we focus on the interview process. They listen to each other's meditation sittings, in small groups of four to six people, and inquire about what they hear. They are restrained from giving advice, interpreting experiences, and trying to lead the meditator to what they think the meditator should know about him- or herself. They do not probe or pry or engage in a lengthy analysis of what they think is going on inside the meditator's mind.

They are taught to respect people's boundaries, if they haven't learned that already, and often reflect upon occasions where they may have crossed a boundary, such as asking a question that was too personal or disregarding what the other person was saying in favor of their own interpretation. They are given feedback on their interviews from both the interviewee and the others in the training group, including me. They become aware of what they have not experienced in meditation and what they know very little about, and how to listen to such experiences in others and inquire with interest. None of them is expert in all the possible experiences meditators can have, but each of them has come to value knowing more about the experiences of others in meditation as a way to further their own learning and meditation practice.

All of the teachers either belong to the Skillful Meditation Project Teaching Sangha, which is the guild of Recollective Awareness meditation teachers, or are part of a smaller group of teachers-in-training who meet on a regular basis. The guild and the smaller groups both abide by a code of professional ethics and are obligated to speak of any transgressions to the other members in the group. These groups also work on interpersonal conflicts, teacher-student issues, difficulties or concerns regarding things I have done (or any other person who has power in the organization), and ways in which to improve the teaching of Recollective Awareness.

Many of the teachers offer their services in the spirit of *dana* (generosity) and do not ask a set fee. Some may have a set fee for certain teaching activities but otherwise teach on a donation basis. I teach solely on a donation basis and will have a fee for workshops and retreats only where money is needed to rent rooms and pay for food, charging only enough to cover those expenses.

Working with a Teacher

In the earlier chapters of this book, I included some fictionalized interviews with me that faithfully represent a type of interview (mostly number one in the following list) you may have with a

Recollective Awareness meditation teacher. There are three main types of interview we engage in:

1. Awareness
2. Empathy
3. Exploration

An awareness interview is one where the teacher asks questions to help broaden the student's awareness of her experiences in meditation. The purpose of this kind of interview is to bring into clearer focus aspects of one's experience that are in the background or on the periphery of awareness. It is our way of teaching greater awareness of both the process one is going through in meditation and the content that comes up with it. So the interview will include what someone was thinking about as well as how she was relating to the thinking. What gradually develops over time with this kind of interview is improved recall of what happens in meditation, more information about one's inner world in meditation, and thus more familiarity with one's experiences while they are occurring in meditation.

An empathy interview is one where the teacher responds with appropriate feeling and understanding to what the student reports. Sometimes being asked too many questions about one's experiences can feel as if one were being interrogated or subjected to scrutiny, and that can be especially disturbing when someone is experiencing emotional pain or distress, where kind and understanding words are more suitable. So when someone does report an emotionally distressing meditation sitting, the interview often begins with empathy for what the person is going through. Teachers in this approach do not report their meditation experiences to students but will occasionally share a similar experience they have had when it serves the purpose of the interview.

The benefit of this kind of interview is that it breaks down some of the sense of isolation and uniqueness people may feel about certain meditative experiences and replaces it with a sense of having a shared (or common) experience of which at least one other person has an understanding. This kind of empathy supports an explorative interview.

What exactly goes on in an explorative interview is hard to pin down. Both the teacher and the student are engaged in exploring an experience from the meditation sitting, and often there is no need to have the exploration reveal something in particular or produce a certain insight. Instead the conversation may fan out in various directions and take in some relevant connections between experiences. Sometimes these interviews go off track, and sometimes they may move in the direction of psychotherapy (particularly if the teacher is a trained therapist as well). But I do try to teach ways for teachers to keep such interviews on track and avoid swerving into psychotherapy.

One way to keep the interview focused on what happened in the meditation sitting is not to ask questions that are about the person's life outside the meditation sitting. So if somebody talks about feeling anxious and having thoughts about eating as a way to quiet or soothe the anxiety, the teacher would ask questions about those thoughts in the sitting and would not inquire about similar thoughts outside the sitting. The direction of the interview would be to explore how the person related to those thoughts, what he saw in the thinking, how it was fueled, and whether it led to any intentions to act on it afterward. The meditator might offer some of his history around such thoughts and how they have come up in his life, but the teacher would not ask about such things, for that would be moving the interview in the direction of counseling, where the teacher might give advice, which is something we may do only in extreme circumstances. The interview could end with no resolution around eating issues for the person, because that is not the purpose of these interviews. Instead, from an explorative interview, the meditator might then be able to meditate with thoughts about eating when he feels anxious and find them to be interesting in new and unforeseen ways and perhaps better understand the conditions for such thoughts. It might also occur that by talking about having such thoughts in meditation, and taking an honest look at them with the teacher's assistance, these thoughts may be tolerated and explored during meditation when they arise on their own.

This is just the tip of the iceberg of what the interviews with Recollective Awareness meditation teachers can be like. There are many dimensions to the interviews, and each one is unique, as we do not use formulaic questions or any type of standardized procedure for interviewing. The questions arise out of careful attentive listening to the student's reporting of his or her experiences in meditation and are meant to facilitate the student's trust and confidence in his or her meditative process and not to foster a strong dependency on the teacher.

At their heart, these interviews are a dialogue with another person, who can be the Good Friend the Buddha's recommends. Each teacher regards these interviews as sacred conversations that are to be honored and kept entirely confidential.

Sending a Meditation Journal to a Teacher

The most common way of working with individual students, outside of a retreat setting, is by the student's e-mailing his or her meditation journals to the teacher, who will then arrange a phone conversation. I have done this with a couple of hundred students over the past fifteen years. Some people do it once and decide it is just not right for them, while others send me a meditation journal once a month for several years. You can try it without any commitment to continue past the first interview and see if it does facilitate your daily meditation practice. All that is required is that you meditate a few times a week and journal at least one of those meditation sittings. It is best to send two weeks to a month's worth of journal entries for the first interview. The entries can be any length and written in any way you like. Some people write in standard paragraphs with complete sentences, while others may just jot down a few phrases of what they remember, and yet others may make a list or a mind map or include drawings. When I or one of the other teachers receives a journal, we then set up a time to talk on the phone or over the Internet. We do not respond to journals in an e-mail because we need to ask more questions and gain a better understanding of a person's meditation practice before making any comments.

Other Ways of Working with a Teacher

Over the past decade, especially with advancements in technology, it has become easier and more satisfying to have interviews over the Internet. I have been able to meet with groups and individuals in other countries and have engaged in some serious and lengthy discussions on meditation practice.

Another way we can offer teaching from afar over the Internet is group interviews when a group has decided to sit together. This can be as a class that is run either on a weekly or biweekly basis for a couple of months or on a monthly basis for a group that would like to meet for six months to a year, or longer if interested. Since there are many possibilities for meeting over the Internet, we are open to exploring any way that might work for people.

If you are interested in contacting me or any of the teachers I have trained, our e-mail addresses can be found on these two websites:

www.skillfulmeditation.org
www.recollectiveawareness.com.au

AFTERWORD: MEDITATION
RESEARCH AFTERTHOUGHT

As a meditation teacher, my interest in scientific research is primarily to expand and increase people's understanding of their own mind in meditation, and possibly from that, to contribute to the general understanding of the human mind in meditation. Contributing to the general understanding of the mind/brain is more appropriately in the domain of scientific research than in the domain of meditation teaching. As much as meditation teachers like me would love to say we know how the brain works in meditation, we can't, since we don't have access to the technology or means to investigate brain functioning. All we have access to is the reports of meditation students and our own subjective ways of referencing their experiences. This is not a small thing, as it can help individuals understand their own subjective experience and become more aware of it, but it is not sufficient for saying how the human mind works.

There have been studies on particular meditation practices that have been used to support the claims of those practices. I think we are at a place where the effectiveness of meditation is no longer in question—it can no longer be considered an idle waste of time, navel gazing, an escape from reality, or whatever notion the uninformed may have had in decades past. Simply, meditation is good for you. The different practices provide general results for most people, such as reduced blood pressure and stress levels, and specific results in the areas the meditation practice trains the mind in, such as awareness, concentration, and compassion. Those who have been meditating for some time have known these benefits, and studies just add validity to what we have already found to be so. They are often deemed necessary for a meditation practice to enter the secular world of hospitals, schools, and government agencies.

What I am interested in are studies that can be used to expand our knowledge of the mind/brain. When a research paper or a book on brain science challenges some views I have or, conversely, corroborates what I have observed and thought, it prompts me to take a look at my mind in meditation from another angle.

Over the years, I have had conversations with Dr. Baljinder Sahdra, who is a psychology researcher. Among other things, she works on the Samatha Project, which is one of the most comprehensive studies on meditation conducted so far. And she has also attended a couple of my retreats and worked with me on her own meditation practice, so she is familiar with this approach to meditation and how it might be researched.

Recollective Awareness meditation could be studied in the same ways that most other meditation practices are being studied. People could be given questionnaires to fill out before and after attending a workshop or retreat. They could be tracked over time beyond the retreat with additional surveys. They could be compared with a control group. They could be subjected to fMRI scans of their brain and other physiological tests, just as in any other meditation practice. Such tests might give more credence to the health or psychological benefits of this practice, or they may show something else (but I doubt that, for if this approach were unhealthy for some of its practitioners, I would have seen that by now—research, in this sense, often confirms much of what is already perceived by astute observation, for such observation is one of the tools of research).

According to Dr. Sahdra, scientific research on meditation done so far has not focused on moment-to-moment choices people make in meditation sittings. That is, for instance, we don't know if stress reduction in mindfulness-of-breathing practices occurs because of the choices people make to be aware of the breath or if it has more to do with the choice to sit still and relax or a choice to disengage from other activities. In the same vein, we don't know how often someone who practices awareness of breathing is actually aware of her breath in the meditation sitting and how much time she is thinking about things, listening to sounds, or drifting into some pleasant sleep-like state. For the most part, researchers have not systematically documented how the research participants are actually meditating from session to session; they just assume the meditators are following the instructions they were given as best they can.

When it comes to an open meditation practice like Recollective Awareness meditation, where the meditator could be doing any number of things in her meditation sittings, the researcher does not have a single instruction to fall back on. What is causing the effects of the meditation sitting? Is it the sitting posture, the openness, the gentleness, the kind of awareness that is being developed, or the interest in one's experience? There is no way for a researcher to identify a single process that could be driving the changes people experience, possibly because there are multiple processes interacting to bring about the changes. Even interviewing the meditators may be confusing, as they could describe different things going on in their sittings that could be contributing to reported calm and well-being. An open meditation practice makes it impossible to find a single cause for one's experience, which is as things should be.

When I talked with Baljinder about this, she concurs that even in most meditation research, where participants are instructed to do a particular practice, such as mindfulness of breathing, there is no way to prove that the instruction alone is causing the results one sees from meditation (because there could be many other psychological processes operating despite the instructions to follow the breath). And yet that is how such research is often interpreted.

I would like to see more of the public interest in meditation re-search go in the direction of understanding how the human brain works in meditative states. What are some of the meditative states that are commonly experienced and how do these affect brain func-tion? It would be good for us to expand our knowledge of what goes on in meditation and how it affects us physically and psycho-logically, rather than trying to prove the validity of one technique over another. What is missing from people's understanding of medi-tative states is that they are human states of consciousness that are ar-rived at through a variety of paths and are not restricted to one particular technique or teaching.

Recollective Awareness meditation can play a greater role in such research, as subjects trained in this approach will be able to remember more parts of their experiences in their reports and be able to provide fuller details. There is also greater curiosity in this approach to meditation, which comes with the freedom to allow one's meditative experience to unfold naturally and move in di-rections that may not be allowed by other practices. And last, since Recollective Awareness meditators can become extremely adept at recalling and describing their meditative experiences, they may aid researchers in learning more about states of mind that form receptively.

One direction that is commonly followed these days by medi-tation writers is the use of research to make statements about what meditation practices are good for the brain. On the surface this appears to be an aid to meditators, but when you look more closely at this tendency, it is driven by biases and speculations on the part of the writer. This is not what scientific research is about. Researchers, by that very name, are skeptics. They are not out to prove people's statements but to explore the nagging unanswered questions, the mysteries that defy superficial explanations.

I would like to see meditation writers use scientific research—for almost every book on meditation will have to cite research at some point or other—to get people to explore their meditative experiences in more depth. I have not done that in this book, at least not in the text itself; instead, what little I have read in the field of brain research has prompted me to take another look at some of my ideas and teachings on the nature of awareness and conceptualization, and to explore them more thoroughly in my meditation sittings and during my interviews with students.

BIBLIOGRAPHY

Anālayo, Bhikkhu. *Satipaṭṭhāna: The Direct Path to Realization.* London:Windhorse Publications, 2004.

Aronson, Harvey B. *Buddhist Practice on Western Ground: Reconciling Eastern Ideals and Western Psychology.* Boston: Shambhala Publications, 2004.

Batchelor, Stephen. *Living with the Devil: A Meditation on Good and Evil.* New York: Riverhead Books, 2004.

———. *Confession of a Buddhist Atheist.* 1st ed. New York: Spiegel & Grau, 2010.

Bodhi, Bhikkhu. *The Connected Discourses of the Buddha: A New Translation of the Saṃyutta Nikāya.* Somerville, Mass.: Wisdom Publications, 2000.

Collins, Randall. *The Sociology of Philosophies: A Global Theory of Intellectual Change.* Cambridge, Mass.: Belknap Press of Harvard University Press, 1998.

Foucault, Michel. *The Order of Things: An Archaeology of the Human Sciences.* New York:Vintage Books, 1973.

Fronsdal, Gil. *The Dhammapada: A New Translation of the Buddhist Classic with Annotations.* Boston: Shambhala Publications, 2005.

Gay, Peter. *Freud: A Life for Our Time*. New York: Norton, 1988.

Gethin, Rupert. *The Buddhist Path to Awakening*. London: Oneworld, 2001.

Gombrich, Richard F. *What the Buddha Thought*, Oxford Centre for Buddhist Studies Monographs. London: Equinox Publishing, 2009.

Gombrich, Richard F., and Obeyesekere, Gananath. *Buddhism Transformed: Religious Change in Sri Lanka*. Princeton, N.J.: Princeton University Press, 1988.

Griffiths, Paul J. *On Being Mindless: Buddhist Meditation and the Mind-Body Problem*. La Salle, Ill.: Open Court, 1986.

Hamilton, Sue. *Early Buddhism: A New Approach: The I of the Beholder*. Richmond, Surrey: Curzon, 2000.

Hanson, Rick, and Richard Mendius. *Buddha's Brain: The Practical Neuroscience of Happiness, Love, and Wisdom*. Oakland, Calif.: New Harbinger Publications, 2009.

Jayatilleke, K. N. *Early Buddhist Theory of Knowledge*. London: G. Allen & Unwin, 1963.

Johansson, Rune. *The Psychology of Nirvana*. London: G. Allen & Unwin, 1969.

———. *The Dynamic Psychology of Early Buddhism*, Scandinavian Institute of Asian Studies. London: Curzon Press, 1979.

Kabat-Zinn, Jon. *Coming to Our Senses: Healing Ourselves and the World through Mindfulness*. New York: Hyperion, 2005.

Kalupahana, David J. *The Principles of Buddhist Psychology* (SUNY series in Buddhist studies). Albany, N.Y.: State University of New York Press, 1987.

———. *The Buddha's Philosophy of Language*. Ratmalana, Sri Lanka: Sarvodaya Vishva Lekha Printers, 1999.

Kockelmans, Joseph J. *Phenomenology: The Philosophy of Edmund Husserl and Its Interpretation*. Garden City, N.Y.: Anchor Books, 1967.

Kohut, Heinz. *The Analysis of the Self: A Systematic Approach to the Psychoanalytic Treatment of Narcissistic Personality Disorders*. Chicago: The University of Chicago Press, 2009.

Kuzminski, Adrian. *Pyrrhonism: How the Ancient Greeks Reinvented Buddhism*. Lanham, Maryland: Lexington Books, 2008.

Masterson, James F. *The Search for the Real Self: Unmasking the Personality Disorders of Our Age.* New York: Free Press; Collier Macmillan, 1988.

Matilal, Bimal Krishna. *Perception: An Essay on Classical Indian Theories of Knowledge.* Oxford: Clarendon, 1986.

McMahan, David L. *The Making of Buddhist Modernism.* Oxford; New York: Oxford University Press, 2008.

Nāgārjuna, and Stephen Batchelor. *Verses from the Center: A Buddhist Vision of the Sublime.* New York: Riverhead Books, 2000.

Nāgārjuna, and David J. Kalupahana. *The Philosophy of the Middle Way: Mūlamadhyamakakārikā* (SUNY series in Buddhist studies). Albany, N.Y.: State University of New York Press, 1986.

Ñānamoli, and Bodhi. *The Middle Length Discourses of the Buddha: A Translation of the Majjhima Nikaya.* Boston: Wisdom Publications, 1995.

Nyanaponika. *The Heart of Buddhist Meditation (Satipaṭṭhāna): A Handbook of Mental Training Based on the Buddha's Way of Mindfulness.* York Beach, Maine: Samuel Weiser, Inc., 1988.

Olendzki, Andrew. *Unlimiting Mind: The Radically Experiential Psychology of Buddhism.* Boston: Wisdom Publications, 2010.

Ricœur, Paul. *Freud and Philosophy: An Essay on Interpretation.* New Haven, Ct: Yale University Press, 1970.

Ronkin, Noa. *Early Buddhist Metaphysics: The Making of a Philosophical Tradition.* New York: Routledge, 2005.

Rorty, Richard. *Philosophy and the Mirror of Nature.* Princeton: Princeton University Press, 1979.

Rossi, Ernest Lawrence. *The Psychobiology of Mind-Body Healing: New Concepts of Therapeutic Hypnosis.* 1st ed. New York: W.W. Norton, 1986.

Sayadaw, Mahasi. *Practical Insight Meditation: Basic and Progressive Stages.* Kandy, Sri Lanka: Buddhist Publication Society, 1971.

———. *The Satipatthana Vipassana Meditation.* San Francisco: Unity Press, 1971.

Sayadaw U Pandita, U Aggacitta, and Kate Wheeler. *In This Very Life: The Liberation Teachings of the Buddha.* Boston: Wisdom Publications, 1992.

Schumann, Hans Wolfgang. *The Historical Buddha: The Times, Life, and Teachings of the Founder of Buddhism.* New York: Arkana, 1989.

Siegel, Daniel J. *The Developing Mind: Toward a Neurobiology of Interpersonal Experience.* New York: Guilford Press, 1999.

Siff, Jason. *Seeking Nibbana in Sri Lanka.* Thamel, Nepal: Vajra Publications, 2008.

————. *Unlearning Meditation: What to Do When the Instructions Get in the Way.* Boston: Shambhala Publications, 2010.

Sperber, Dan. *Metarepresentations: A Multidisciplinary Perspective, Vancouver Studies in Cognitive Science.* New York: Oxford University Press, 2000.

Stede, William, and Rhys Davids, T.W. *Pali-English Dictionary.* New Delhi: Oriental Books Reprint Corp., 1975.

Stern, Daniel N. *The Present Moment in Psychotherapy and Everyday Life* (Norton series on interpersonal neurobiology). New York: W.W. Norton, 2004.

Thanissaro, Bhikkhu. 1997. *Vitakkasanthana Sutta: The Relaxation of Thoughts (MN 20),* translated from the Pali. Access to Insight: www.accesstoinsight.org/tipitaka/mn/mn.020.than.html

Thera, Kheminda. *Path, Fruit, and Nibbana.* Colombo, Sri Lanka: D. Roland D. Weerasuria, 1965.

Thera, Ñāṇavira. *Clearing the Path.* Colombo, Sri Lanka: Path Press, 1987.

Thera, Soma. *The Way of Mindfulness.* 3rd ed. Kandy: Buddhist Publication Society, 1967, 2003.

Torey, Zoltan. *The Crucible of Consciousness: An Integrated Theory of Mind and Brain.* Cambridge, Mass.: MIT Press, 2009.

Vajracharya, Dunda Bahadur. *Majjhima Nikaya.* Nepal: Bir-Purna Pustak Sangrahalaya, 2001.

Walshe, Maurice. *Thus Have I Heard: The Long Discourses of the Buddha (Digha Nikaya)* London: Wisdom Publications, 1987.

Wegner, Daniel M. *The Illusion of Conscious Will.* Cambridge, Mass.: MIT Press, 2002.

Zunshine, Lisa. *Why We Read Fiction: Theory of Mind and the Novel.* Columbus, Ohio: Ohio State University Press, 2006.

Index

harm, 140, 171
harshness, 7–9, 11
hatred, 67, 75, 98, 152, 163–64
heart, 19, 97, 163–64, 197
hindrances, 12, 82, 92–93
hope, 120, 135–37
hopelessness, 41, 83, 88, 121, 129–30
humility, 163, 190
hurt, 86–87, 109, 140, 150

identifying with, 63, 83, 183–84
ignorance, 109, 171
illusion, 117, 124, 152, 188
imagination, 103–5, 134–35, 138
immaturity, 191–92
impasse, 175
impatience, 9, 26, 35, 128–29
impermanence, 102, 186–88
inner (internal)
    conflict, 160–61, 175
    critic, 7, 74, 137, 159, 182
    dialogues (conversations), 47, 116,
        124–26, 138–39, 144
    monologues (voice), 19–20, 80,
        110–11, 138
    world, x, 6, 10, 47, 113, 151–52, 157
innovation, ix, 150
Insight meditation, 59, 102, 156. See also
    mindfulness
insights, 14–15, 61, 88, 161, 190–91, 196
integrity, 183–84
intention, 10, 13, 62–63, 104, 123–29, 164
interest, 7–9, 14, 78, 117, 174, 194
interpersonal relationships, 47–48, 148,
    194
interpreting experiences, 55, 70, 193
irritation, 8, 61, 113, 133, 172
isolation, 47–48, 192, 195

journey, 3, 43, 75, 132
judging, 2, 14, 101–2, 128

karma, 135, 181
kindness, 7–9, 52, 75–77, 159, 164
knowledge, 64, 69, 154, 169, 179, 202

laziness (lethargy), 9, 20, 88, 92
learning, 9, 49, 134, 144, 149, 172–73
liberation, 89, 95–96, 146, 183–85, 189,
    192

linearity, 73, 108–11, 116–20, 170–71, 182
list making, 90, 125–27
listening, 1, 14, 17, 105, 149, 193–94, 197
logic, 65, 93–94, 107, 153, 181
loneliness, 8, 51, 119–20
love, 91, 199
loving-kindness, 52, 54, 75–77
lust, 2, 67, 83, 88–90, 163, 192

mantra, 6, 37, 160
materialism, 89, 134, 175
maturation, 191–97
meditation. See Recollective Awareness
    meditation
meditation research, 165, 199–203
meditation sittings, 22–31, 109–10, 118–
    19
meditative states, 46, 94, 178, 202
memories, 1, 69, 123, 137, 140–44, 157,
    177–78
mental illness. See anxiety; depression
metaphors, 80, 111, 115, 176, 185
microanalytic interview, 166–67, 171
micromanaging, 7, 164
middle way, 48, 75–76
mindfulness
    bodily movements, 100, 106
    breath, 11–13, 18, 27, 34, 76–81,
        110–11, 201
    sensations, 6, 18, 39, 68, 81, 111
    senses, six, 101, 107–8, 112–13
    thoughts, 102–5
mind/body, 190
mind/brain, 165, 199–200
momentariness, 181
monkey mind, 3
monks, 5, 91, 136, 146–49, 173–75, 180
multilinear present moment, 116–22

narratives, 15, 48, 97, 141, 151–52, 178–
    79, 189
negative thoughts, 7, 11, 37, 77, 130–31,
    162–64
nibbana, 146, 180, 184–88, 191
nimitta (sign, theme, object), 76
nirodha, 188
nonattachment, 84, 134
nonconceptual, 44, 102, 188–89
no-self, 82, 181, 186–88
nostalgia, 142